Christian
Growth
Through
Meditation

Beyond "Transcendental Meditation"

Christian Growth Through Meditation

Fay Conlee Oliver

CHRISTIAN GROWTH THROUGH MEDITATION

Library of Congress Cataloging in Publication Data

Oliver, Fay Conlee.
  Christian growth through meditation.

  Bibliography: p. 121.
  1. Meditation. 2. Christian life—1960-
I. Title.
BV4813.O44   248'.3   76-23252
ISBN 0-8170-0716-4

To the members of the Foothills Meditation Group who have blessed this effort with patient listening, suggestions, resource materials, experimentation, prayer, and friendship. My love and gratitude to you all.

Preface

My purpose in writing this book is to introduce meditation as a tool for spiritual growth both to Christians individually and to the leaders in the Christian church. Meditation is a practice that will enable the Christian to achieve definite, rapid, sometimes electrifying progress in his or her inner life. Although I go into more detail in the book concerning why a Christian should meditate, I will say here that it enhances the time-honored practices of Christian prayer, worship, study, and service.

We can talk about God, sing songs praising him, worship what we know of him, and even serve him in various ways, but if we have no direct experience of his presence, he is to us only an idea. Meditation enables the Christian to move from "believing" to "knowing." Through meditation we can learn how to "be still and know that I am God." We experience what we have only talked about before.

Meditation is not new and has been a part of many cultures for thousands of years. It is a technique that carries no body of belief in itself. The meditator can believe any or no religion, though there are few, if any, atheist meditators. It is only when a level of consciousness is reached, which is known as cosmic consciousness, bliss consciousness, and other terms, that the meditator realizes a oneness with everything and a unity with God. This concept is applicable to any religion. Meditation carries no other theological overtones and can be practiced by fundamental or liberal Christians, Protestant or Roman Catholic Christians, or any other kind of Christian.

Many books on meditation are much more detailed than this one. None that I know of aims so directly at the possibilities for Christian use of this tool. Although I have included a broader picture of meditation, I have directed my efforts to stating with simple clarity why a Christian should and how a Christian can meditate with life-changing results. My intention is to give to Christians and to the Christian church an accurate accounting of a spiritual technique of immense value.

Meditation is spreading rapidly today in the Western world. This phenomenal interest is evidence of a deep spiritual hunger. Most who seek to learn meditation today must learn it outside the Christian church. Those who teach it independent of any Christian basis promise that meditation will bring relaxation, relief from stress, happiness, greater clarity of purpose, and efficiency. Christian meditation offers all this and more. Paul said it in 2 Corinthians 4:6, "For God, who said, Let light shine out of darkness, has shone in our hearts . . ." (translation by George M. Lamsa, A. J. Holman Company). Meditation can help us to wake up to this great Christian truth. It is a method for growth the Christian church should not ignore.

Acknowledgments

I would like to express appreciation to my brother-in-law, Howell D. Boyd, whose interest and urging were key factors in my beginning this book; to the Reverend Charles M. Bezdek, my pastor, who read the manuscript in progress and encouraged me to continue; and to my husband, Earl, my most helpful critic. To all the authors of writings to which I have referred, I acknowledge my indebtedness.

Contents

CHAPTER 1

Meditation: What Is It?

Meditation has come to America. Its beginnings, marked with excited endorsement by famous entertainers, some of whom rushed off to India for more intensive study, suggested a fad that would soon fade away. The surprise today is that, over a decade later, interest and participation in meditation continue to grow steadily, and at present literally hundreds of thousands of Americans—students, business executives, professional people, blue-collar workers, housewives, and others—meditate daily. But what is it? What is this practice called meditation?

Some words, like love, are used in too many ways to be definitive. Meditation is such a word. It has been used to mean a devotional talk, the act of sitting silently, a few printed words of inspiration, or a period of concentrated thought. None of these definitions fits the procedure with which this book is concerned. The understanding of the word in our country is changing as the practice of meditation becomes increasingly widespread. Formerly it meant a general type of contemplation. Today equal importance is given to its Eastern definitions suggesting an inner awakening in the silence of oneself.

The inner stillness is one of two frontiers for exploration that excite humankind today with promise for transforming human life. The other, of course, is the reaches beyond our small planet Earth, space with its vast possibilities. But the investigation of the complex regions within human beings themselves is perhaps the greatest adventure still available.

Both interests are ancient, for when haven't human beings wanted to go to the moon and beyond, and when haven't they pondered who they were, why they were here, and what they could and should do? But today there is a breakthrough in both fields in knowledge and in the projected use of this knowledge. We have sent men to walk on the moon, and now we look far into a space future for which Neil Armstrong's "giant step for mankind" was truly only a baby step. And scientists, now, not just farsighted mystics and poets, are recognizing the unknown and undeveloped possibilities within human beings themselves.

Research on the complexity and potentiality of the human brain is verifying the faith in our mental and spiritual abilities long held by ancient spiritual masters. One researcher is Dr. Robert Ornstein, research psychologist at Langley Porter Neuropsychiatric Institute in San Francisco, California, and teacher at the University of California Medical Center. His most pertinent work concerns the two sides of the brain. The left half, he states, is responsible for logical and intellectual thought, as well as for a sense of time. The right side is more intuitive and appears to handle creative concepts and expressions. His findings are discussed in his book *The Psychology of Consciousness,* which attempts to reconcile science and mysticism. He makes the case that our contemporary scientific approach has been to amplify the logical-rational half at the expense of the other area. Many of the esoteric disciplines, he believes, are actually training regimes for the brain's intuitive hemisphere.[1]

Today in the fields of psychology, biology, chemistry, and physics, scholarly thoroughness is being used to examine areas of unexplained behavior, intuition, and unusual or paranormal phenomena previously dismissed as outside normal scientific investigation. There is tremendous new interest in the power of the mind. A new day is dawning as we become more knowledgeable about our real abilities.

The practice of meditation with which this book is concerned is a means for helping a person understand these abilities better as a part of an expanded awareness for the purpose of spiritual growth. The

Christian may believe firmly in his or her spiritual nature, but may not always know how to realize it consciously so that his or her total life can be lived abundantly. Meditation is a tool for developing a new state of awareness or consciousness. For the Christian, it can be a pathway toward greater awareness of his or her inner self, his or her spiritual being.

As defined in the literature about Transcendental Meditation, the method brought to this country from India by a Hindu monk, Maharishi Mahesh Yogi, meditation is a "fourth major state of consciousness, as natural to man as the other three physiologically defined states—wakefulness, dreaming, and deep sleep."[2]

Psychologists, since the early days of Freud, Jung, and others, have talked about other states of consciousness, particularly about the unconscious aspects of the thinking processes. The subconscious and the unconscious are common words in our present vocabulary. It is everyday knowledge that we are often motivated by emotions, experiences, and memories that lie deeply buried within our brain, not always easily accessible to conscious thinking.

Meditation has to do with levels of consciousness of which we are not habitually aware in our usual daily lives. Basically, to bring the definition into a smaller framework, it can be described as an experience which transcends the normal thinking processes to another level of awareness and in some cases ultimately to a consciousness of the unity of God and persons. Meditation involves the totality of a person and therefore that part which we as Christians consider primary, the spirit, already linked intimately with the Spirit of God.

Research has verified that meditation moves a person into a definite physical state different from all other physical states. In this country, research in the field of meditation began with Dr. R. Keith Wallace, physiologist, and Dr. Herbert Benson, cardiologist and associate professor at Harvard Medical School. Their studies show that the meditative state is different from the other known states of existence; sleep, dreaming, and wakefulness. They found that meditation produces a state of deep relaxation, though the subjects remain awake and alert. Subjects studied showed lower body metabolism and decreases in heart and respiratory rates. During meditation, oxygen consumption decreased (indicating less stress), and the lactate ion concentration in the blood (believed to be a partial cause of stress feelings) decreased; skin resistance increased markedly (indicating a decrease in anxiety), and there was an increase in intensity of "slow" alpha waves (indicating a relaxed, comfortable state of mind and body).[3] This and later research confirms that the meditative state involves a definite difference in the physical state; it is not an illusion engendered by a rash of literature on the subject.

If a person in meditation is in a different state of consciousness from his normal wakeful consciousness, yet is fully alert, what can be said of this state? One of the better explanations is given by Maharishi Mahesh Yogi in his book *The Science of Being and Art of Living*. Maharishi, a physicist before he became a monk, was for thirteen years the disciple of a Hindu Master, His Divinity Swami Brahmananda Sarawati. The most illustrious of the Jagadguru Shankaracharyas of India, this Master is known for reviving practices from the ancient Vedic tradition. In his book, Maharishi explains the difference between the meditative state and the wakeful state as the difference between being in the absolute and relative states of existence. He calls that which is never-changing, unmanifested, and eternal as the absolute state and calls that which is ever-changing, relative, and active as the relative state. Like the ocean which is silent at the bottom and perpetual motion at the surface of its waves, yet is the same ocean, so being is being whether in the relative or absolute state. He also likens this phenomenon to the difference in the ways hydrogen and oxygen atoms are arranged in different phases. In one phase they show the properties of gas; in another, water; and another, ice. Yet, though gas, water, and ice are all different, the basic ingredients hydrogen and oxygen are always the same.

He says that persons in the wakeful state are in the relative state in which things are constantly active and changing. But during meditation they move into or toward the state of the absolute where things are never-changing and absolute. As they practice meditation, they experience more and more subtle states of thinking as they move into the absolute state, and the relative state changes because of these experiences.[4] However, it is only at the level called cosmic consciousness that they can be fully aware of themselves in the absolute state.[5] More is said of cosmic consciousness in a later chapter.

This then explains the difference between meditation and prayer. Although it is no doubt possible for prayer to move a person into another state of consciousness, for the most part prayer is an expression of the relative state. It is experienced in the wakeful state, as an outpouring of our thoughts to God, an outgoing of thoughts and energy. By contrast, meditation is an ingathering of energy and awareness. Meditation has been called listening and prayer termed talking to God. Although they are both ways of relating oneself to God, they are on different levels of consciousness. This is in no way labeling prayer as secondary. Prayer is a primary experience in spiritual growth which meditation only enhances. As meditation is practiced, prayer changes. It is elevated to that which comes from God; it becomes an outpouring of our deepest self to that which is holiest. Our prayers become worthy of the deepest and highest within us.

A simple experience of something often clarifies a definition more than exhaustive language. So, although further descriptions of various methods of meditation will be given in a later chapter, for clarification a simple form of meditation that can be tried by the reader immediately will be offered here.

The first step is to make sure you are not disturbed. Find a quiet place and take the telephone off the hook. Although people who have meditated for years may be able to meditate in the middle of a noisy subway, the beginner should have quiet for learning. Sit in a comfortable chair with a fairly straight back. Place your feet on the floor. Settle yourself so your body is comfortable; it is to be forgotten. To set the mood and elevate the thoughts, devotional material, such as a section from the Bible, may be read. This introductory lesson will be divided into two ten-minute parts, a period of concentration followed by a period of meditation, a practice used in several types of meditation.

The main benefit gained from the period of concentration is learning to control one's thoughts, to center the thinking. The difficulty of this will become obvious during this initial period. It is a surprise to most people to see how scattered and hard to corral their thoughts are. After observing what little jurisdiction we have over that mass of ideas, emotions, dreams, and words whirling around in our heads, we should be less surprised that our lives show the results of this lack of mastery of our mental machinery.

For this exercise in concentration, choose an object, either one within sight or in your mind, such as a flower, cross, or candle, or choose an idea or word, such as humility, brotherhood, or the kingdom of God. Choose anything that has symbolic value to you.

Let your mind dwell on what you have chosen. Any thought related to your choice, its symbolism or related implications, is acceptable during this period. When other thoughts come, as they will, gently let them go, and bring your mind back to the point of concentration.

For illustration, I will choose a rose. I see it in a vase on a table across the room. It is a loose yellow bud in the beginning stages of opening. I look at it and appreciate it for its beauty. A sense of wonder comes to me along with the words of the poet about beauty as its own excuse for being.[6] The odor reaches me faintly, and I breathe deeply to catch more. The yellow-orange shade reminds me of a sunset that thrilled me on a vacation last summer. I relax, remembering the unfettered feeling of that five-day period. I think of the rustic cabin by the lake, rented for those few days of freedom from routine. The memory of a casual restaurant down the road comes with the smell of one particularly delicious lobster dinner. I then realize that I am no longer concentrating on the rose. I look again at the flower. I see the way the outer petals are relaxing to allow the entire blossom to unfold. This suggests a parallel in life, as we relax and let the inner beauty of our thoughts and our true self planted by God shine forth. I am reminded that much care went into the cultivation of the rose-bush to allow it to grow into a healthy plant that could produce such perfect flowers. This suggests to me the care necessary for each life.

Such is the way our rambling thoughts come and go, but they can be centered for this block of time at one point of concentration. Some forms of meditation use a sound for focusing the attention, enabling the meditator to move into a deeper level of consciousness.

After the exercise in concentration, the next phase, which follows without interruption, is the period of meditation. If your eyes have been open during concentration, close them now. Sit in silence for ten minutes allowing thoughts to flow freely. Do not make any effort to think or not to think. Thoughts will come; allow them to come and go without any attempt at control. You will feel yourself relax, physically and mentally. As the muscles can be relaxed by flexing and relaxing, so the mind during this meditation period will move more easily into the meditative state because of the period of concentration preceding it.

After the ten-minute meditation period has passed, gently bring your thoughts back to the level of your surroundings. As you become more experienced in meditation, you will usually sense the length of the time period, though time is somewhat distorted in meditation. Until then, just glance at a handy watch or clock.

You may find that coming out of meditation is similar to waking from a deep sleep, with the exception that your mind has been fully alert all the time. If your hands or feet tingle or feel cold, a little movement soon restores them to normal. Do not hurry to return to normal activity. It takes time to go into and to come out of the subtler levels of consciousness. It is a shock to the system to come out too quickly, and although this will do no harm, it is not the most pleasant way to end meditation. Allow several minutes for this transition to take place. You may find that you are so relaxed you would enjoy a few minutes of sleep. If a bed or sofa is handy, use it. This is a temporary drowsiness resulting from complete relaxation, but it is not the prelude to a deep sleep. You will awaken in a few minutes with extra energy with which to pursue your tasks.

Meditation, especially as practiced by Christians, is only a means to an end. Although enjoyable in itself, it is not for the purpose of experiencing some kind of psychic high, akin to drug use. Although various degrees of relaxation and sensation are realized, and levels of ecstasy are sometimes experienced, the meditation experience itself is not the reason for practicing it. The important change is in the lives of the persons meditating. Persons who meditate regularly day after day will find several things beginning to happen. Their days will become more efficient and productive. Their purposes will become clearer. The work that they want to do, they will do more easily. They will gain a sense of peace in their daily lives and will find their interest in spiritual things growing. The purposes of their lives may change in accordance with new spiritual insights. They will find an increasing ability to love.

Since the results of meditation are beneficial and immediate and produce initially at least three pluses—more energy, efficiency, and tranquility—it would seem worth trying. No thought need be given to any ecstasy or level of consciousness termed "cosmic" or "bliss," which may take years to achieve. If and when this comes, it is a bonus and doesn't negate the initial advantages of earlier stages of meditation. Like any art or technique, meditation must be practiced for increased benefits. But meditation is helpful from the beginning. Jesus told us to judge something by its fruits. As persons practice meditation, they find the fruits of meditation in their lives. Persons withdraw in order that they may become more purposefully and efficiently active. They meditate in order to wake up to life. For Christians, it is the larger life to which they are awakening. Meditation is only a tool for this larger purpose.

Notes to Chapter 1

[1] Robert Ornstein, *The Psychology of Consciousness* (San Francisco: W. H. Freeman and Company, Publishers, 1972), pp. 96-99.

[2] R. K. Wallace, "The Physiological Effects of Transcendental Meditation," Ph.D. Thesis, University of California, Los Angeles, June, 1970.

[3] Robert Keith Wallace and Herbert Benson, "The Physiology of Meditation," *Scientific American,* vol. 226, no. 2 (Feb., 1972), pp. 85-90.

[4] Maharishi Mahesh Yogi, *The Science of Being and Art of Living* (London: Allied Publishers Private Limited, 1963), pp. 33ff.

[5] *Ibid.,* p. 273.

[6] See "The Rhodora," in *The Portable Emerson,* Mark Van Doren, ed. (New York: The Viking Press, 1967), p. 315.

CHAPTER 2

Why Should
a Christian
Meditate?

Ours is an age facing the ominous threat of technological development capable of world annihilation in addition to nuclear stockpiling, world pollution, overpopulation, energy and food shortages. One hopeful aspect in such a time is the emerging of many groups purposing to develop resources of human potential through new research and practical application. A cataloging of such organizations on just the West Coast reads like the makeup of a new utopia. Many, of course, will be short-lived, and many will neither delve into the deeper needs nor provide real answers. But some offer impressive hope for a continuance of new breakthroughs in knowledge and use of this knowledge for the growth of humankind.

Dr. Edgar D. Mitchell, the sixth astronaut to walk on the moon, founder and president of the Institute of Noetic Sciences, one of the more promising of the new research organizations, says:

I believe that civilization is in a critical state and mankind is at an evolutionary crossroad. On one hand problems and conflicts have arisen which are global in scale and have brought society to a condition of escalating planetary crises. On the other hand, man's potential for creative change, fulfillment, and benevolent control of his environment have never been greater.

I believe that both problems and potentialities are ultimately a function of human consciousness—i.e., there will never be a better world until there are better people in it. The most effective and enduring way to resolve the problems and to realize the potentialities is through the enlightenment of individuals.

I believe that man's consciousness is *the* critical factor in the future we will build for ourselves.[1]

It should be gratifying to us in Christian churches that research from the academic community is finding more and more promise in the human faculty. It should renew our faith in our religious heritage. Almost two thousand years ago, Jesus was teaching of human potential. "You are the salt of the earth. . . . You are the light of the world. A city set on a hill . . . a lamp . . . on a stand, and it gives light to all in the house" (Matthew 5:13-14). His analogies tell one after another of the significance of human life. Enabling that life to develop was recorded as his primary purpose. "I came that they may have life, and have it abundantly" (John 10:10). His efforts to help people experience the abundant life, to know truth, to tap resources which produce love, joy, and growth constituted his ministry.

Christians still claim this message of potentiality, which, when translated into living, offers us today, as in the first century, our greatest pathway for growth.

These same purposes constitute a central reason for the church's existence, helping people find these resources for abundant living. We generally refer to this process as Christian growth, and it is a lifelong work. Paul frequently writes of the need for Christian growth, once calling new Christians in Corinth, "babes in Christ," saying, "I fed you with milk, not solid food, for you were not ready for it" (1 Corinthians 3:2).

Of all the old or new organizations in existence today working to develop human potential, it is still the church that possesses the message of the necessary resource, God's power at work within us. The church brings hope for change and growth because it begins with the assumption of our spiritual nature, an assumption ignored in most secular plans for change.

The traditional means for growth offered in our churches are worship, prayer, study, and service. All are basic in any plan for Christian growth. Meditation is not able to replace any of them. But none is adequate without the touchstone of an inner awareness. Meditation can help the Christian reach the quiet essential to awaken spiritual awareness. And it should enable us, as we touch the deepest within, to use each of the traditional means of growth in ways more worthy of our best selves.

Prayer has been de-emphasized in our churches for the past decade or two. The old type of prayer meeting, along with a dependence on prayer, is mostly a posture of the church of the past. It is not yet known whether the present wave of charismatic meetings, which do emphasize prayer, will change this picture. We do know that we still need prayer, but perhaps, like the early disciples, we realize that we also do not know how to pray. Our prayers are too frequently ego-centered and childish, instead of childlike in humility. When through meditation we reach into the soul of our soul, our prayers change as our lives do. Meditation should help us to turn again to prayer with more of the Christlike spirit.

Reaching into the silence to experience the presence of God is not new in Christianity. Our heritage, from its beginnings in the Jewish religion, has always acknowledged silence as a way to realization of God's presence. The Old Testament is full of the connection between quiet and the cognizance of God. In Psalm 46, the psalmist tells us to "Be still, and know that I am God." As in many other passages, we find again in Isaiah (40:31-41:1),

> But they who wait for the Lord shall
>   renew their strength,
> They shall mount up with wings like
>   eagles,
> They shall run and not be weary,
>   they shall walk and not faint.
> Listen to me in silence. . . .

The New Testament shows Jesus following that tradition. Time after time the Gospels, as in Mark 1:35, record that Jesus rose early and went apart by himself. The disciples, in looking for him, might find him on a hill, in a boat, or on the other side of the lake.

It was on an unaccompanied trip to a mountaintop that Moses received the Ten Commandments; Paul withdrew to Arabia to assess his Damascus experience; and it was alone in the garden of Gethsemane that Jesus faced the looming destiny of the cross.

Although traditional and current Christian thought encourages seeking quiet for spiritual growth, there is little need for reminders of the difficulty of finding quiet in today's society. There is a constant onslaught of noise from the radio, television, telephone, dishwasher, washing machine, traffic on the street and in the air, the blare of our neighbors' activities, as well as our own. Research is showing increasing evidence that noise is physically and psychologically harmful. But this is only one of the difficulties.

The noise from without can only be matched by the noise from within ourselves: our involvement with our activities, tensions over responsibilities, anxieties about someone we love, memories that haunt, plus the trivia that clutter our larger purposes. Even when we succeed in shutting out the noises from around us, we still have to deal with the confusion from within.

Where can we go to escape the noise both external and internal? We can go deeper within; through meditation we can move into the quiet center of ourselves. As persons experience the level of the meditative state, they realize that meditation is a truly possible and efficient way of reaching that deep inner quiet capable of changing their capacities, direction, energies, and perhaps most important and interrelated to all, their thoughts.

Jesus put major emphasis on thought, equating it in consequence to action. It must have been shocking to the people of his day to hear his statements in Matthew 5:

> You have heard that it was said to the men of old, "You shall not kill; and whoever kills shall be liable to judgment." But I say to you that every one who is angry with his brother shall be liable to judgment; . . . You have heard that it was said, "You shall not commit adultery." But I say to you that every one who looks at a woman lustfully has already committed adultery with her in his heart (Matthew 5:21, 22, 27, 28).

These are still shocking statements today, even though modern psychology is teaching the underlying unity between a person's thoughts and actions. Jesus taught that thoughts are the results of an inner condition. Changing the condition results in changed thoughts and consequently in changed action.

In his essay "The Over-Soul" Ralph Waldo Emerson said: "We live in succession, in division, in parts, in particles. Meantime within man is the soul of the whole; the wise silence; the universal beauty, to which every part and particle is equally related; the eternal ONE."[2]

In pointing out the necessity for right thinking, Jesus gave us not only a standard of perfection but a plan for moving toward that goal; right action becomes the result of first getting the inner self into a state of loving harmony.

We cannot deal with Jesus' teachings about anything so basic, however, without considering the concept that constituted the bulk of and the focus for his teachings, the kingdom of God. Many volumes have been written about this concept, including a master's thesis on the subject by this writer. This term has been interpreted differently by different New Testament scholars. The late Georgia Harkness, in her recent book, *Understanding the Kingdom of God,* does an excellent job of explaining these various conceptions of the term, which we will not deal with here. However, the spirit characteristic of the kingdom, no matter the interpretation, rises above other deliberations, and it is about the spirit of the kingdom that there is agreement among the scholars. For the overriding spirit of the kingdom is one of joyful, life-changing awareness of God in charge of the world as Immanent Father, Creator, Dispenser of Perfect Justice, and Active Love. Theologians, no matter their understanding of time or place, or how structured, or how initiated, agree that this kingdom is permeated with a particular spirit of love and a new understanding for humankind. It is clear that these teachings about the kingdom were intended to lift humankind's thinking to a new spiritual level. They are therefore directly related to today's consciousness-raising efforts purposing to change behavior for benevolent results.

When the teachings about the kingdom are viewed as lessons about a supreme mental and spiritual consciousness, they are illuminated in a new and exciting way.

The teachings make a connection with doing the will of God, following spiritual goals instead of material, having a singleness of purpose, manifesting loving concern through action, and being like a little child.

George A. Buttrick interprets the last to mean being dependent and trusting, friendly and unconscious of rank, candid, receptive to life and its wonder, and in a state of innocent purity.[3]

Many of the teachings about the kingdom are about the nature of its growth. The parable of the mustard seed and the parable of the leaven are twin parables illustrating the same idea, large results from small beginnings (Mark 4:30-32).

Jesus taught that the kingdom of God is of such value that it can be compared to the pearl of great price (Matthew 13:45, 46) and the treasure hid in a field (Matthew 13:44). It is pictured as worth the supreme cost necessary to obtain it.

Have we strayed from our purpose for this chapter, to state clearly why a Christian should meditate? I think not. If this spiritual consciousness, this awareness of God's rule, permeated with love, joy, and justice is worth all to find, we should use whatever practices make possible our finding it. For we are told to "seek first his kingdom" (Matthew 6:33), though it comes as a gift from God when it comes. Through meditation, the Christian can seek a new level of spiritual consciousness, this kingdom of God.

The first three Gospels tell us that at the beginning of Jesus' active ministry he withdrew for a lengthy period to the quiet of the wilderness. There, alone, he faced the inner choices common to all who seek spiritual growth; he faced the temptations to let materialism, fame, and worldly power direct the course of his life. It was in the quietness that he found the wisdom to turn away from selfish ego gratification to determine to worship only God and to serve only the coming of God's kingdom.

Few of us can retire to a wilderness for forty days. We need a way to find quietness even in the middle of an active, noisy life in this country.

Considering the difficulties of and the necessity for experiencing that deep inner quiet, meditation becomes a valuable method, one worth incorporating into the lives of Christians and a procedure that should be taught in our churches, the one place meditation is having a slow start in contrast to the rapid growth outside the church.

Much of the expansion of interest in meditation can be attributed to the efforts of the Transcendental Meditation organization. Although this has spearheaded the movement, other groups that teach meditation also report growing interest in the practice. Although there is a beginning interest today, Christian churches have until recently ignored the movement.

Church membership has decreased in the last decade. Interest, if judged by attendance, has declined. Yet meetings about parapsychology, unconventional healing, development of human potential, and meditation are well attended. This seems to indicate that something is missing in our churches. That which seems to be promising new meaning for life, personal help, and wider horizons is emerging outside the institutional church. The church, still caught up in a socially relevant activism, continues to deemphasize the mystical aspects of its heritage, though, in truth, the two can never be separated with impunity.

Another reason for the hesitancy toward meditation in our churches is its link with Hinduism, Buddhism, and other Eastern religions. Aware of the trust in the revelation of Jesus Christ,

Christians, until recently, have too automatically assumed that anything outside the teachings of the Christian church is erroneous. Fortunately, that situation is changing today. Paul reminded the ancient Greeks that God does not leave himself without a witness, and it is the nature of persons to seek the truth of God. The great religions of the East have truths of God also.

God's truth permeates all of life, outside the church as well as inside. But it is essential that the church, if it is to offer spiritual light and strength to its age, give priority to the things of the spirit.

Any movement concerned with the expansion of human consciousness, that promises new inner awareness, and new spiritual depth, should be welcomed by Christians and Christian churches. As the church tries to move persons from a secular, materialistic outlook to a holy, God-centered consciousness, it should give full support to a technique that can help them move deeply into the silence of themselves and there encounter meaning, for it is in silence that persons encounter God.

Notes to Chapter 2

[1] Edgar D. Mitchell, "A Personal Message to You from the Sixth Man on the Moon," uncopyrighted promotional brochure, Institute of Noetic Sciences, Palo Alto, CA 94301.

[2] Brooks Atkinson, ed., *The Selected Writings of Ralph Waldo Emerson* (New York: Random House, Inc., 1950), p. 262.

[3] George A. Buttrick, ed., *The Interpreter's Bible,* vol. 7 (New York: Abingdon Press, 1951), pp. 467-468.

CHAPTER 3

The Christian Heritage in Meditation

As a Christian practices meditation, he or she experiences an affinity with others, both living and in history, who have looked for God in the silence and have shared the insights and larger purposes that emerged. In Christian history it is the mystic whose experiences we recognize as most resembling those of the meditator.

Although the words "mystical" and "mysticism" are often misunderstood and, perhaps for this reason, neglected and even avoided terms, most Christians have had some kind of mystical experience. For, in its simplest definition, mysticism means experiencing the presence of God. This shows most of us to be at least embryonic mystics, for whether on a mountaintop surrounded by majestic white peaks and snow-laden pines or during a regular Sunday worship service, we have known something of the love and majesty of God in a way we cannot adequately describe. It is at least in part hunger for this heightened awareness of the divine that keeps us moving in our Christian endeavor.

Yet the words "mysticism" and "mystical" are often confused with the terms "mysterious" and "magical" and with anything not well understood and hazy, and are sometimes linked with experimentation into the occult. These terms are alien to us today. We associate them with long-robed monks praying in cloistered cells, cut off from ordinary affairs and from most human contact. And this picture comes with good reason, for some mysticism in church history was the way of the ascetic hermit. These ascetics served a purpose in the development of Christianity, and we do not minimize their contribution.

However, it may come as a surprise to learn that the active mystic who withdraws for periods of spiritual nourishment to return to productive work in the world is more common in the history of Christianity. Evelyn Underhill, in her authoritative book, *Mysticism,* states that "All records of mysticism in the West . . . are also the records of supreme human activity."[1]

It is with these mystics that meditators feel at home. It is in the tradition of active mysticism that meditation follows. A rich heritage of literature produced by such mystics gives us guidance, assurance, and joy. As we read it, we are delighted to find that they were discovering similar, even identical truths, whether they lived in the first or fourteenth century; they were discovering the same insights that begin to come to us through meditation and which are so badly needed today.

A working definition of mysticism is given us by Rufus M. Jones, who did so much to expound mysticism in the early twentieth century. He calls it, "the type of religion which puts the emphasis on immediate awareness of relation with God, on direct and intimate consciousness of the Divine Presence. It is religion in its most acute, intense, and living state."[2]

William James classifies an experience "mystical" when it is: (1) "ineffable" (defies expression); (2) "noetic" (transfers knowledge, insights); (3) "transient" (short-lived); and (4) "passive" (as though grasped by a greater power).[3]

The terms "mystical" and "mysticism" come from a Greek word "mystae" used to designate the initiates of the mystery religions, believed to be recipients of a vision of the gods and a higher life.[4]

There are lengthier and more complex definitions, but these are adequate and should assure the reader that we are not talking about any avenue into the occult. They should also remove some of the strangeness of the subject, for we can fit our personal experiences of closeness to God within their boundaries.

At the heart of all the great world religions, and certainly in Christianity, mysticism is the lamp that carries the oil. It is based on the assumption that intuitive knowledge of reality and direct conscious contact with Ultimate Reality or God are possible. If it is possible for us to meet God so that we are conscious of this meeting, the fulfillment of religion is this point of contact. As God is Spirit, this meeting is neither subject to scrutiny in the laboratory nor even adequately expressible in language.

Miss Underhill points out repeatedly in her book *Mystics of the Church* that the mystical experience is the very soul of religion and that "no Church in which it is not present truly lives."[5] She states, "All the knowledge of God which is possessed by men has come to us in the last resort through some human consciousness of Him."[6]

This would suggest that the history of the Christian church must then include at its center the history of the mystical experience, and when we look at the lives of the shapers and periodic revitalizers of the church, we see this verified.

Before we review briefly the mystic strain in church history, let us look for a moment at the levels of the mystic states and in particular at the ultimate mystical experience. There is a vast difference between the feelings of closeness to God we frequently feel in church and the ultimate mystical experience, also called cosmic consciousness and other names. These ultimate experiences are rare but, even if known only once or occasionally, are considered by those who record them as pinnacles for an entire life. It is that most intense experience, that "direct and intimate consciousness of," the confirmation for which the mystic strives.

Other lesser mystic experiences, although not so overwhelming or intense, are still valued by the mystic. Most who wrote of their experiences recorded their progress through various stages before realizing the final confirmation.

An important reason for studying the efforts of the mystics is to compare them with our efforts and progress in Christian growth. Their writings convince us that meditation, or contemplation as they usually call it, can produce steady spiritual progress. By looking at their experiences, we see the possibilities for change in our own lives.

There are no categories into which we can put our records to assess our growth, even with the standards of the mystics for comparison. We cannot say that we are in Class III or some such designation because we have had this or that happen and have felt such a way. But we can look at the histories of a few mystics and search for parallels and lessons that will help us grow as we meditate.

We can see our potentiality as we study the life-changing experiences at all levels, including the ultimate experiences of "direct and intimate consciousness of God."

It would seem logical to look at the beginning stages of the mystic's development because such levels more nearly resemble ours. Yet, the ultimate experiences have elicited more complete records, and the descriptions of them usually include discussion of lesser states of awareness including the initial and continuing efforts toward the final goal. So, in a sense, we get a panoramic view of the valley and the ascent to the mountaintop.

The peak experience we are concerned with is called by various terms: "cosmic consciousness," "bliss consciousness," "enlighten-ment," "illumination," "Christ consciousness," "the ultimate experi-ence," and others. *The Highest State of Consciousness* edited by John White gives thirty-three excerpts from various writers discussing this highest state. Abraham Maslow describes this state clearly in his *Religion, Values and Peak-Experiences.*

An excellent study of these ultimate experiences is found in the book *Cosmic Consciousness* by Dr. Richard M. Bucke, a Canadian psychiatrist of the last century whose thinking on this subject was greatly respected by William James, Evelyn Underhill, and other great thinkers. Dr. Bucke became interested in this state of consciousness not because of any interest in mysticism, religion, or meditation, but because he was interested in the mental evolution of humans and saw these extreme experiences of consciousness as higher forms in the evolutionary process. He viewed the evolutionary process as having gone through three definite stages of consciousness. The first stage produced the perceptual mind of the lower animals, who could receive only sense impression. The second was character-ized by that of the higher animals, the receptual mind with its simple consciousness. Finally came the conceptual mind of human beings, accompanied by self-consciousness. He regards the experience of "Cosmic Consciousness" as a fourth state. It is summarized by G. M. Acklom in his introduction to Bucke's book.

> The new, fourth stage of consciousness, which enables man to realize the oneness of the Universe, to sense the presence in it and throughout it of the Creator, to be free of all fears of evil, of disaster or death, to comprehend that Love is the rule and basis of the Cosmos—this is Cosmic Consciousness, which, Bucke prophesied will appear more and more often until it becomes a regular attribute of adult humanity.[7]

Although these peak experiences of consciousness are not identical from person to person, there is agreement or similarity in a number of factors. The mystics' records confirm the findings of Dr. Bucke. They report a sense of the universal purposes and the all-rightness of those purposes, a conviction of the nearness of God, an awareness of beauty, power, and splendor of the larger life. A great sense of reality, truth, is perceived, accompanied by an overwhelming feeling of joy and love. Light, and sometimes heat, is present. Voices and visions are sometimes heard and seen. And, finally, a new purpose is retained by the individual as he or she tries to attune his or her life to his or her new vision of reality.

This, then, is the confirming experience of consciousness described by Christian mystics as well as others. Some of the cases studied by Bucke came to this experience in ways other than meditation. However, the history of Christian mystics, as well as those mystics from Buddhism, Hinduism, and other religions, shows that meditation is a pathway that can lead to the experience. It is indeed the highest possibility toward which meditation can carry us.

Let us look at a recent example of this kind of confirming experience. Dr. Edgar D. Mitchell tells about his experience as an astronaut on his flight to the moon.

> It began with the breathtaking experience of seeing planet earth floating in the immensity of space—the incredible beauty of a splendid blue-and-white jewel floating in the vast, black sky. I underwent a religious-like peak experience, in which the presence of divinity became almost palpable, and I *knew* that life in the universe was not just an accident based on random processes. This knowledge, which came directly, intuitively, was not a matter of discursive reasoning or logical abstraction. It was not deduced from information perceptible by the sensory organs. The realization was subjective, but it was knowledge every bit as real and compelling as the objective data the navigational program or the communications system was based on. Clearly, the universe has meaning and direction—an unseen dimension behind the visible creation that gives it an intelligent design and gives life purpose.[8]

Although those who have experienced this final stage of consciousness agree that there is "direct and intimate consciousness of the Divine," there is considerable variation in their understanding of it. Some feel that they have taken the initiative for the encounter. Others feel they are responding to an initiative taken by God. Some describe the experience as a oneness, a unity with God; others talk about communion, fellowship. For some, there seems to be a loss of personality as it merges with God. Others view it as a heightening of personality through the presence of God. As all maintain the difficulty of expressing the essence of the event, and as we would expect variety among different individuals, this variation in the description of this experience is not surprising.

The less spectacular occasions of mystical awareness of God contain many of these same elements. The difference seems to be in the breadth of the final experience and the intensity with which the entire spectrum of awareness hits the individual.

To give form to these ideas, let us look at them in the lives of a few who greatly affected the history of the Christian church, starting with the two most responsible for its beginnings.

Jesus cannot be omitted in any discussion of New Testament mysticism without ignoring essential facts about him. If, as some scholars feel, the teachings about the kingdom of God concern a new level of spiritual consciousness and relationship with God, then these teachings are about the mystic way. A basic premise of the church from its beginnings, through the Protestant Reformation, the Counter-Reformation, and into the present is that Jesus is the incarnation of the Spirit of God, the unity of God and humankind in a person, a mystic union which is the foundation of the Christian faith. That Jesus lived in awareness of God's presence is not in question.

Two out-of-the-ordinary experiences of Jesus have all the indications of being ultimate mystic states. The first is his baptism by John the Baptist at the Jordan River. In Matthew 3:16 and 17 we read:

> And when Jesus was baptized, he went up immediately from the water, and behold, the heavens were opened and he saw the Spirit of God descending like a dove, and alighting on him; and lo, a voice from heaven, saying, "This is my beloved Son, with whom I am well pleased."

The second is recorded in Matthew 17:1-5:

> And after six days Jesus took with him Peter and James and John his brother, and led them up a high mountain apart. And he was transfigured before them, and his face shone like the sun, and his garments became white as light. And behold, there appeared to them Moses and Elijah, talking with him . . . and a voice from the cloud said, "This is my beloved Son, with whom I am well pleased; listen to him."

Since this is reported through the eyes of the disciples, there are three ways the story could be interpreted; as a mystical experience they were witnessing, one they were sharing, or one which was exclusively their own.

However, following each of these occasions, Jesus' life took a different direction. After the first, he went into the wilderness to contemplate the course of his life and ministry. Following the second, he set his face toward Jerusalem to end his physical ministry on a cross.

It is in the Gospel of John that the mystical union of Jesus with God is featured. Since John's Gospel was written after Paul's ministry and writings, we shall look at Paul before considering this mystical literature.

Paul, one of the outstanding mystics of any age, is the first Christian mystic about whom we have a great body of information. The fact that Paul is credited with being the first and probably the greatest missionary, the shaper of Christian theology, and the great organizer of the early church should not blind us to the fact that his beliefs and his teachings resulted from mystical experiences. These experiences are referred to throughout his writings. The first such happening changed his life's purposes and direction completely. This was the familiar conversion experience on the road to Damascus.

Paul was born as Saul, a Roman citizen of Jewish parents in Tarsus, a city under Roman rule in Cilicia. He studied in Jerusalem under the famous rabbi Gamaliel and became a strict Pharisee, that group dedicated to the purity of the Jewish faith through keeping the religious laws. As a young man, he was thoroughly dedicated to serving the Jewish religion and at the time of his conversion was involved in the persecution of the followers of Jesus. Acts 8:3 refers to Paul's part in this activity. "But Saul was ravaging the church, and entering house after house, he dragged off men and women and committed them to prison."

Paul was traveling the road to Damascus on instructions from the high priest, "that if he found any belonging to the Way (of Jesus), men or women, he might bring them bound to Jerusalem." The rest of the story is best recorded in Acts 9:3-9.

> Now as he journeyed he approached Damascus, and suddenly a light from heaven flashed about him. And he fell to the ground and heard a voice saying to him, "Saul, Saul, why do you persecute me?" And he said, "Who are you, Lord?" And he said, "I am Jesus, whom you are persecuting; but rise and enter the city, and you will be told what you are to do." The men who were traveling with him stood speechless, hearing the

voice but seeing no one. Saul arose from the ground; and when his eyes were opened, he could see nothing; so they led him by the hand and brought him into Damascus. And for three days he was without sight, and neither ate nor drank.

In Paul's story we find a number of factors frequently present in the peak experiences. He was blinded for three days by the sudden presence of an intense light. He heard the voice of Jesus, and received a new vision of reality. Acts does not specifically refer here to the joy and love almost always accompanying such cases, but Paul's subsequent enthusiasm and references suggest their involvement. Certainly he gained a new perception of Jesus.

Paul began restructuring his life immediately after this dramatic event. Acts tells us that after several days of being with the disciples at Damascus, he proclaimed Jesus in the synagogues, saying, "He is the Son of God" (Acts 9:20).

In Galatians we are told that he went to Arabia to reassess his life's purposes and direction in the light of his new convictions.

The letters of Paul to the churches attest to his mysticism as much as the accounts of his first dramatic experience. Georgia Harkness in her book *Mysticism: Its Meaning and Message* says that although Paul is acknowledged as the first great theologian of the church, his theology does not stem only from reasoned argument or external evidence, but "rests on the inner witness of the Spirit, which he had experienced and which he believed others should experience for the transformation. . . . It is this note of inner witness, not conjured up from within but imparted through Christ, which is the groundwork for Paul's Christ-mysticism."[9]

For Paul, the way of salvation is to be "in Christ," a term used interchangeably with the "Spirit of Christ," the "Spirit of God," the "Spirit of Jesus Christ," the "Holy Spirit," and the "Spirit." When you are "in Christ" you are a new creature, and the new creature has spiritual insights, "And we impart this in words not taught by human wisdom but taught by the Spirit, interpreting spiritual truths to those who possess the Spirit" (1 Corinthians 2:13).

Paul attributes his ministry to this new spirit. "I have been crucified with Christ; it is no longer I who live, but Christ who lives in me" (Galatians 2:20). He was deeply aware of a new being, the union of himself with Christ.

Along with Paul's letters, the Gospel of John and the book of First John stand as literary monuments to the mystical beginnings of

Christianity. The Gospel of John shows the deep mystical union between God and Christ, referring to God as the Father of Christ, Love, Light, and Spirit. It is in the incarnation that these qualities are made known to humanity, for the Son is the manifestation of God.

The underlying concept of the union of God and Christ is extended to humankind in the vine passages of John. "I am the true vine, and my Father is the vinedresser. . . . I am the vine, you are the branches" (John 15:1, 5).

The same sense of mystic union is present in First John. Chapter 4, verses 12 and 13, are a clear statement of this: "No man has ever seen God; if we love one another, God abides in us and his love is perfected in us. By this we know that we abide in him and he in us, because he has given us of his own Spirit."

Now let us look briefly at the mystic strain in church history following the first century beginnings to see the major role the great mystics played both in the shaping and revitalization of the church. It is beyond the bounds of this book to deal with the history of mysticism in any exhaustive way; in fact, we cannot do justice to the subject, for those throughout the centuries who lived close to God influenced the times in which they lived and the ages following in a way we can hardly imagine. An excellent book for obtaining an overview of their lives and influence is Evelyn Underhill's *The Mystics of the Church.* We will look at only a few as examples to show that the contemplative life is the soul of the church and a pattern we can imitate with confidence. We will also look at some of the great lessons to be learned as we follow a similar pathway.

Church historians give a special place to Augustine (354–430). Dr. Williston Walker says of him:

> In Augustine the ancient church reached its highest religious attainment since apostolic times. . . . all Western Christianity was to become his debtor. . . . He was the father of much that was most characteristic in medieval Roman Catholicism. He was the spiritual ancestor, no less, of much of the Reformation. His theology, though buttressed by the Scriptures, philosophy, and ecclesiastical tradition, was so largely rooted in his own experience as to render his story more than usually the interpretation of the man.[10]

His conversion at the age of thirty-two followed a worldly, sensuous life. He tells about his inner conflict between urges toward the higher and lower planes of living in the first sections of his *Confessions.* His resolution of this conflict is summarized with his words. "You shone, you scattered my blindness . . . you touched me, and I burned for your peace."[11]

We think of him as a man of action, as he was. Five years after his conversion he became a priest and the assistant bishop of Hippo; four years later, the bishop of Hippo. This was during a time of great controversy in the African church. His life is a great example of action combined with contemplation. The church as it developed under his leadership attests to his involvement with the practical, for his is a record of skillful leadership. The *Confessions* and his other writings show the centrality of the mystical experiences that shaped him as he shaped the church.

We skip over so many who deserve mention to Francis of Assisi (1182–1226). Walker says of him: "In Francis of Assisi is to be seen not merely the greatest of medieval saints, but one who, through his absolute sincerity of desire to imitate Christ in all things humanly possible, belongs to all ages and to the church universal."[12] His life and work were monumental testimony to the power of Christ's message and greatly contributed to the renewal of the church. His story is well known. He was the son of a well-to-do merchant and in his youth was primarily interested in mischief and revelry, but after his conversion became the joyous, nature-loving, contemplative imitator of Christ, founder of the movement that became the Franciscan order of the church.

One of the amazing examples of the power of the mystic is that of Catherine of Siena, Italy, whose name is not as well known as our other two examples, but who held a place of power and spiritual influence in her time as few others have. She was born at a time of almost unparalleled ecclesiastical degradation of the church, the fourteenth century. The politics of the papacy had reached a new low, and the Pope was in exile in Avignon. The church hired mercenary troops for the purpose of war; the priesthood was corrupt. As there was little spiritual leadership from the church, a network of mystical lay groups emerged to fill the void. The groups usually formed around some practicing mystic who, without leaving the church, was a force of spiritual strength.

In Germany, during her childhood, the movement of the Friends of God was at its height; in England the followers of Rolle continued his work; in Italy Giovanni Columbini, a rich Sienese merchant who had embraced utter poverty, was founding the congregation of the Gesuati, which sought to revive the simplicity and ardour of St. Francis, and caused a considerable reformation among the friars; whilst St. Bridget of Sweden (1303–1373), a mystic of the type of St. Hildegarde, was pouring forth apocalyptic prophecies and political denunciations at Rome.[13]

Into such a world came the religiously precocious girl Catherine. At the age of sixteen she became a Sister of Penance of St. Dominic, made up of women who followed a religious role in their own homes. She secluded herself for three years in a small bedroom of her father's house, and with a total concentration on the inner life, her mystical powers developed quickly. This period was culminated in an experience known as her "mystical marriage with Christ." She then returned to an active life and was able to exert tremendous energy in countering the corrupt practices of the times. She carried on an active ministry to the poor and sick, a preaching ministry to the unconverted, and she exerted pressure on the politics of the times. "Her one desire was to bring about a peace in which the Christian life could flourish and the spiritual authority of the Church could be restored."[14] It was she more than any other who influenced Pope Gregory XI to return to Rome. In addition to all her busy involvement with the practical, we have her *Divine Dialogue,* an account of the direct teaching she received in contemplation. She is another example of how the union of action and contemplation resulted in a life of power. She died at the young age of thirty-three.

We have only given a few examples to show the contribution of the mystic personality in shaping and revitalizing the church. We could go through the centuries, and just naming them would fill a book. Many know of the contributions of St. Ignatius of Loyola, St. Theresa of Avila, and St. John of the Cross in countering the low state of the church during the period of the Spanish Inquisition. Also familiar to many are the names of Meister Eckhart, Brother Lawrence, Jan van Ruysbroeck, Jacob Boehme, and George Fox. Not so familiar are thousands of others who lived the contemplative life and constituted the inner life of the church, no matter the century.

Let us just mention one twentieth-century mystic, though there are many from whom to choose. Frank Laubach (1884–1970) is known best for his work in literacy. It is estimated that his "each-one-teach-one" method for teaching illiterates resulted in the literacy of over sixty million persons in over three hundred languages, and thereby changed their lives economically, psychologically, and socially. He was invited to bring his program to many countries and received many honors for his work. He attributed his success to the presence of God in his life. He, like Brother Lawrence so many years before him, tried to keep God in his thoughts constantly. He says:

> This concentration upon God is *strenuous,* but everything else has ceased to be so. I think more clearly. I forget less frequently. Things which I did with a strain before, I now do easily and with no effort whatever. I worry about nothing, and lose no sleep. I walk on air a good part of the time. Even the mirror reveals a new light in my eyes and face. I no longer feel in a hurry about anything. Everything goes right. Each minute I meet calmly as though it were not important. Nothing can go wrong excepting one thing. That is that God *may slip from my mind* if I do not keep on my guard. If He is there, the universe is with me. My task is simple and clear.[15]

It would be interesting to review other such lives, but even the study of these few mystic giants makes several conclusions possible.

The development of the inner life does not happen in a vacuum. The life of contemplation and meditation flourishes best within the environment of the church. Miss Underhill points out that the mystic needs the church, and the church needs its mystic center. Mysticism is not all of religion. It needs to be part of history, dogma, and the institution to reach the sense-conditioned human. "Man needs a convention, a tradition, a limitation . . . and this convention the mystics find best and most easily in the forms of the church to which they belong."[16]

Another obvious lesson we learn from the lives of mystics is that growth comes in stages and takes effort and time. Paul spent time in Arabia before he began his active ministry following his Damascus experience. Miss Underhill marks a passage of nine years in Augustine's development between the time of his conversion and "the whole of that interior growth which turned the fiery and tormented convert into the solid man of prayer, able to take 'the food of the full grown.'"[17] Catherine of Siena spent three years in confinement working on her inner life before she began her active ministry.

Another important conclusion is that attention to the inward quest can occur amid conditions not especially congenial to such an endeavor. We often postpone this important part of our Christian development thinking that at some less busy time in our day or life we will begin a life of prayer and meditation. When we view the activities of the great mystics, many of whom were also great church administrators, we realize that this inner life is not only possible within a busy schedule but perhaps is the source of power that makes the other efforts effective.

The condition of a saintly church also is not essential, for we see how frequently in the periods of greatest church laxity the mystic rose to be that inner pure light that would not die no matter the setting in which it burned.

Another message from these mystics, repeated over and over in their writings, is that the enjoyment of the pleasures of the contemplative state is not the goal. The goal is the greater work that is possible as a result. The mystic withdraws, as does the Christian meditator, for nourishment, rest, spiritual energy, direction, and insight, then returns to the work for which he has been called.

Without exhausting the lessons we can learn from the mystics, we will mention but one other. The contemplative life results not only in the life of power we have illustrated, but also it is the greatest source of happiness. The records of those who have experienced the higher states of mysticism convince one that the attempt to describe the happiness, in spite of exuberant language, falls short of adequately expressing the joy.

In any study of the lives of the mystics and of states of consciousness possible through meditation, two basic questions emerge. Is this, the consciousness of the Divine Presence, no matter how described, real or illusory? If real, what can lead us to such an encounter?

We can determine the reality of an experience at least partially by results. Does the experience move persons toward greater reality in their lives? Does it heighten their awareness? Does it make them more effective in relating to people and events around them? Does it help them realize their potentiality as persons?

For thousands of mystics, from the beginning of religions until today, the validity of the experience was not in question. For them it was intensely real, intensely important, and no attempt at either deceiving themselves or others. But the preponderance of material does not prove validity, for we also know that thousands of disturbed patients in mental hospitals have illusions that to them are equally real. And we know that all of life is built on assumptions we do not attempt to prove, some of which are false. We assume the trustworthiness of laws of nature as we understand them, the reliability of machines upon which our lives sometimes depend, and the worthiness of people we love.

The best test seems to be, as Jesus said, in the results. The mental patient who thinks he or she is Napoleon or believes he or she has spoken with Churchill shows in days following this occurrence no increase in an ability to relate to the real world around him or her. This is the exact opposite of the mystic following a mystical experience. The mystic exemplifies heightened ability to deal effectively with the world around him or her.

St. Theresa of Avila, one of the notable mystics of the sixteenth century, said it this way:

> This may lead you to think that such a person will not remain in possession of her senses but will be so completely absorbed that she will be able to fix her mind upon nothing. But no: in all that belongs to the service of God she is more alert than before; and when not otherwise occupied, she rests in that happy companionship.[18]

Evelyn Underhill, after a lifetime of studying the mystic, says that "only the mystic can be called a whole man, since in others half the powers of the self always sleep."[19]

We have seen this truth in the lives of the examples given. The validating mark of mystics is the increase in their powers; their perception, their knowledge, their self-discipline, their power of will, their acceptance of their tasks and suffering, their powers of endurance, and their effectiveness with and independence of external conditions.

If the reality of the experience can be judged by the results, we still have the question of how to attain such an experience. As meditators, we are particularly concerned with the question, for perhaps it is here that we can see steps in our meditative life that will lead to Christian growth.

Scholars of mysticism record the mystical experience in stages, but most agree with the late fifth- or sixth- century Syrian Christian, Dionysius the Areopagite, who divided the steps into three general classifications.

> ... the Active Life through the Way of Purification, whereby men may become true servants of God; the Inner Life, the Way of Illumination and of real sonship with God; and the Contemplative Life, which is the Unitive Way whereby men may attain to true friendship with God.[20]

As we have seen from our brief look, the mystic has played a central role in the life of the church from its beginnings. What place does mysticism hold in the church today? There are no doubt mystics working quietly as they always have been, and there is a new interest today in the subject of mysticism. But there is as yet little evidence of mysticism becoming central in the church of today. There is some indication that the new charismatic services, the growing interest in the Holy Spirit, and the beginning interest in meditation are evidences of revitalization of the mystic center of the church. But it is too early to see if these movements will change the disinterest which has characterized our churches for so long in recent times.

Dr. Harkness cites several reasons for this lack of interest in mysticism. In the wave of Christian liberalism, the emphasis shifted to rationality and the social imperatives. Then came neoorthodoxy, which taught that God is Wholly Other, a position of opposite assumptions from those of mysticism. The neoorthodox said that God can be worshiped and obeyed, but hardly experienced in intimate communion. Radical theology appeared next, the "God-is-dead" movement, along with teachings that indicated that it was pointless even to talk of God, a position that eliminated a God who could be reached through human consciousness.[21] All these influences are still with us today, and it is in this atmosphere that mysticism wilted, and the movement in meditation, similar to mysticism in purpose and direction, has swept past the church with only a few inside recognizing it as a movement of the Spirit.

Yet much of the mysticism of the past is still with us in our rituals, sacraments, music, architecture, and worship services. Through the Eucharist, the Roman Catholic is made aware of the presence of the Divine. Although Protestants eliminated much that had mystical purpose, the music, prayers, and the sermon are planned with the hope that a Presence will be felt. Unfortunately, sometimes the symbols planned to create awareness of the Divine become a substitute. Instead of a real meeting between God and the person, the ritual, the dogma, the liturgy, the sacraments become central and the experience stops with them.

The Roman Catholic Church still retains the mystic center in the mass. Another denomination with a continuing dedication to meeting with God's Spirit is the Society of Friends, known as the Quakers. This branch of the church resulted from the mystical experiences of George Fox in seventeenth-century England. Fox had an overwhelming experience of God that gave certitude to his life and initiated his ministry of the Inner Light.

From the beginning, the Society of Friends has emphasized the Inner Light. Guided in their living by this light, the Friends have through the years been a bulwark of strength in the struggles for peace, equality, and justice, and in ministering to human suffering.

The church service today, as in its beginning, is centered around the quiet period. Members sit in silence and speak, pray, witness, and such, only as they are led by the Inner Light. They have made a contribution to Christianity and to the world far out of proportion to their small numbers, a testimony to the power of the mystical relationship.

There are other facets of Christianity that are examples of modern-day mysticism. The evangelical denominations have as their central emphasis the conversion commitment made during a period of encounter with God. The growth of these denominations during a period of declining membership in other churches perhaps is due in part to this factor.

Through the ages, the church has survived the societies within which it has existed, as well as its own mistakes, weaknesses, and wanderings primarily because within its framework that essential meeting between God and humankind has taken place. If the church is to survive this day, it must return that mystical meeting to its central place in the life of the church.

Christian meditators, as they follow the tradition of the great Christian mystics and encounter that Divine Light, can become what God created them to be: the salt of the earth, the light of the world, a city set on a hill, a lamp that gives its light to all that are in the house.

Notes to Chapter 3

[1] Evelyn Underhill, *Mysticism* (New York: The World Publishing Company, 1970), p. 173.

[2] Rufus M. Jones, *Studies in Mystical Religion* (London: Macmillan and Co., Ltd., 1909), p. xv.

[3] William James, *The Varieties of Religious Experience* (New York: Random House, Inc., The Modern Library, Inc., 1902), pp. 370-372.

[4] Evelyn Underhill, *The Mystics of the Church* (New York: Schocken Books, Inc., 1964), p. 10. First published by James Clarke & Co., Ltd., Cambridge, England, in 1925. Used by permission of James Clarke & Co., Ltd.

[5] *Ibid.*

[6] *Ibid.,* p. 11.

[7] Richard Maurice Bucke, *Cosmic Consciousness* (New York: E. P. Dutton and Co., Inc., 1962), pp. iv-v.

[8] Edgar D. Mitchell, "Outer Space to Inner Space: An Astronaut's Odyssey," *Saturday Review,* vol. 2, no. 11 (Feb. 22, 1975), p. 20.

[9] Georgia Harkness, *Mysticism: Its Meaning and Message* (Nashville: Abingdon Press, 1973), p. 46.

[10] Williston Walker, *A History of the Christian Church* (New York: Charles Scribner's Sons, 1959), p. 160.

[11] Rex Warner, transl., *The Confessions of St. Augustine* (New York: The New American Library Inc., 1963), p. 235.

[12] Williston Walker, *A History of the Christian Church,* p. 234.

[13] Underhill, *The Mystics of the Church,* p. 153.

[14] *Ibid.,* p. 158.

[15] Frank C. Laubach, *Letters by a Modern Mystic* (New York: Student Volunteer Movement, 1937), p. 24.

[16] Evelyn Underhill, *The Essentials of Mysticism* (New York: E. P. Dutton & Co., Inc., 1960), p. 37.

[17] Underhill, *The Mystics of the Church,* p. 66.

[18] St. Teresa of Avila, E. Allison Peers, trans. and ed., *Interior Castle* (Garden City, N.Y.: Image Books, imprint of Doubleday and Company, Inc., 1961), p. 210.

[19] Underhill, *Mysticism,* p. 63.

[20] Dionysius the Areopagite, *The Mystical Theology and the Celestial Hierarchies* (Nr. Godalming, Surrey, England: The Shrine of Wisdom, 2nd ed., 1965), pp. 18-19.

[21] Harkness, *Mysticism: Its Meaning and Message,* p. 17.

CHAPTER 4

Meditation, Health, and Human Potential

The lives of the mystics show the spiritual heights to which meditation can carry us. But what about the effects of meditation on health and everyday living? Many of us notice changes after starting meditation daily. We feel more energetic, optimistic, and alert. We wonder if meditation can be a positive factor in maintaining health. We wonder if it can directly affect diseased and under-par bodies. We wonder if meditation can help us develop higher powers than we now possess, even if we never succeed in reaching the high states of ecstasy and fulfillment of the mystic.

Dr. Carl Simonton, a radiation therapist, related an intriguing story of meditation and healing at a Stanford University symposium on healing. Dr. Simonton was formerly Chief of Radiation Therapy Service at Travis Air Force Base and is now in private practice in Fort Worth, Texas. His story was of a patient, thirty-five years old, with a carcinoma of the uterus. She had a severe infection at the time of the diagnosis, which caused Dr. Simonton to be pessimistic about the outcome. Two weeks later, her gynecologist reported the tumor smaller in size. Dr. Simonton again examined her after another two weeks and found the tumor decreased by at least 50 percent of its volume. When he questioned her about any change in her life, she gave no adequate explanation. Later Dr. Simonton gave her a procedure of relaxation and imagery that he was introducing to many of his patients. It was only then that the woman admitted using a similar practice in meditation, a technique she had begun after reading of Edgar Cayce's suggestions for meditation.[1]

Dr. Simonton reports many unusual healings of persons using his method of relaxation and imagery. Such stories are also coming from meditators. Meditation meetings are frequently spiced with accounts of improved health. Two recent books give examples of the improvement in health resulting from meditation. *The Healing Potential of Transcendental Meditation* by Dr. Una Kroll, a family doctor, discusses the release of tension through Transcendental Meditation (TM) and the resulting physical improvements. *TM: Discovering Inner Energy and Overcoming Stress,* by Dr. Harold H. Bloomfield, Michael Cain, and Dennis Jaffe, tells of the latest scientific research on TM and its implications for health, psychiatry, and social betterment.

Dr. Bloomfield tells of his results using TM with fifty psychiatric patients. He reports that as patients meditate, conflicts seem spontaneously to resolve themselves without the necessity for probing the various conflicts. He says:

> I've had several patients who began to meditate and six months later it will turn out some conflict that had been a source of great anxiety earlier was almost gone. There might be some lingering trace, but without having worked on it directly, we found that the deep rest of TM allowed that healing process to take place naturally.[2]

He has dealt with mild disorders as well as hospitalized patients with severe psychiatric diagnoses: schizophrenia, manic-depressive illness, and severe characterological problems. He finds that meditation crosses diagnostic boundaries. It produces stability in the nervous system and reduces stress and anxiety, the common denominator in all mental illness.[3]

There is a growing body of research concerning meditation's effects on bodily processes. Most of the research has been on Transcendental Meditation because of the availability of meditators and the uniformity of instruction and practice.

We have already referred to the research initiated in this country by Dr. Keith Wallace which he began in connection with his study of the psychobiology of consciousness for his doctorate at the University of Southern California Medical School. The results of this research and subsequent work with Dr. Herbert Benson have been published in *Science, Scientific American, American Journal of Physiology,* and elsewhere. Other researchers are also exploring facets of the relationship between meditation and health.

To summarize the results of all the findings to date is not possible here, and summaries of this data are readily available. However, a number of facts should be noted again. Research has shown that the following physiological changes take place during meditation: lowered body metabolism reflected by changes in oxygen consumption, carbon dioxide elimination and cardiac and respirator activity, decline in blood lactate, rise in the electrical resistance of the skin, and increased intensity of alpha waves, all reflecting less stress and greater relaxation.[4]

Emotional changes reported are also quite impressive. One study of forty-nine practitioners of TM, using the Freiburger Personality Inventory by Fehr, Nerstheimer, and Torber showed that meditation reduced nervousness, reduced depression, reduced irritability, increased sociability, increased self-assuredness, decreased tendency to dominate, decreased inhibition, increased emotional stability, and increased staying power and efficiency.[5]

In addition to laboratory results, there is other less objective but impressive evidence. One questionnaire returned to Dr. Wallace by 394 persons practicing TM reported the following improvements in their health since starting meditation: 117 noted fewer colds, 29 fewer headaches, 19 a decrease in allergic reactions, 7 an improvement in hypertension conditions, and 84 an improvement or cure of miscellaneous problems, such as overweight, acne, asthma, ulcers, insomnia, and multiple sclerosis, 33 noted an improvement in mental health, and 22 had been able to discontinue psychiatric treatment.[6] *Time* magazine reported on a questionnaire that Drs. Wallace and Benson gave to 1,862 drug users who had been using drugs heavily; they gave these drug users the questionnaire after they had been practicing TM for at least three months. The study showed that most stopped using drugs completely or greatly decreased their use. The longer they practiced TM, the greater was the change.[7]

This brief report does not exhaust the evidence of improvement in health resulting from meditation. But there is a broader picture of health and consciousness relative to the possibilities in meditation. Startling facts are emerging from research that give us clues not only about how to improve our health through meditation but also how to improve our life so that we may live nearer to our God-given potential.

There is a new wave of hope sweeping through our age generated by these discoveries. We are emerging to be far more than we have recently thought ourselves to be. In fact, the message coming to us over and over from this research is that our ideas of our limitations and ignorance of our potential have been a crippling inhibitor in our development. Mr. George Leonard, in an article for *Saturday Review,* states, "It is still clear that we are operating with only a tiny fraction of our true abilities. . . . Thus, science brings us around to a central thesis of most of the world's religions . . . in the King James version of the Bible: 'So God created man in His own image.'"[8]

Three ideas emerging from a great amount of research relative to the possibilities for growth through meditation are: (1) that there exist energies available for healing either from an outside source or from a deeper level inside a person; (2) that the mind has power to control changes beyond our previous knowledge, to an extent we can now only guess, and (3) that consciousness exists on many levels and has implications for life far beyond our present knowledge.

Meditation, as we have discussed earlier, is a technique for moving into deeper, more subtle levels of consciousness. It enables a person to tap a more basic source of energy as well as to release stress and tensions that internally divide and prevent the integration necessary for coherent and forceful thought and action. It is being found to be a practical method for developing possibilities within us that research is uncovering.

Although space limitations prohibit going into the details of research, let us observe briefly some of the implications from this expanding knowledge. Both the breadth of the subjects being studied and the involvement of hundreds of scholars and scientists attest to the growing acceptance for study of subjects once scorned. This new interest and openness is a relief and vindication for the pioneering parapsychologist who for so long led a lonely way. It was only in 1969 that the Parapsychological Association was accepted into the American Association for the Advancement of Science.

Much of the research concerning healing energies has centered around unconventional healing. The term "unconventional healing" is used, not because evidence for change can't be documented by regular scientific procedures or even described in scientific terms, but because at the present time, these practices are outside the conventional procedures used in medicine. Healing practices that fall into this "unconventional" grouping are prayer, laying on of hands, acupuncture, psychic surgery, and mental control. Until recently, the academic community and the medical profession have ignored and sometimes even ridiculed these practices. But today better document-ation and scholarly research on these paranormal healings are causing many doctors to take an honest look at them, even though current ideas in the profession are sometimes challenged. A growing number of doctors and scientists are no longer content to call such healings "unexplained remissions." The Academy of Parapsychology and Medicine in Los Altos, California, founded in 1970 by a distinguished group of physicians and scientists, is doing a pioneering work in the investigation of unorthodox medicine or practices in healing.

Actually, the idea of a life energy, being encountered in most of the healing called unconventional, is hardly new. It has been believed in many cultures since ancient times that human beings are filled with a vital energy or life force. Many also claim that the universe is filled with this energy, and that it is possible for us to attune ourselves to it. The ancient Chinese called it "ch'i"; ancient Egyptians called it "ka"; the Hawaiians, "mana." Hindus believe in an energy which they call "prana," which they claim unifies the total personality: body, mind, and soul. Henri Bergson, the French philosopher, talks about "elan vital," the ultimate creative, vital energy of the universe. Dr. Carl Jung calls the energy "libido"; not the sexual libido of Freud, but a more primal, more fundamental force. And psychics claim to be able to see a force field surrounding a person's body which they call the "aura."

Research studies, such as Sister Justa's with the enzymes, are verifying the existence of these body energies. The reader is encouraged to read a book giving the exciting stories of this research. One such book is *Psychic Exploration: A Challenge for Science* edited by Dr. Edgar Mitchell and John White.

Studies that explain and verify the existence of body energies are interesting to meditators who have already observed an increase in energy since beginning meditation. It is even more exciting to learn of the research in progress concerning the use of this energy through the power of the mind for control of bodily functions and other changes. Again, it is directly related to meditation, for the practice of meditation, as has been stated, releases stresses and permits more integrated and coherent thought and action. The possibility for the use of this forceful power of the mind is an extended potentiality for the meditator, for example, in intercessory prayer.

Prayer is an ancient means of directing healing energies to one in need of them. No mature Christian believes that prayer is a way of persuading God to do something He is reluctant to do. But as we learn more about the healing energies and the power of the mind, we can believe that thoughts move with some strange force from one person to another, not hampered by distance. We become more earnest about praying when we believe that we can truly serve as channels for this healing energy to reach its destination. With exceptions here and there, the main line churches have neglected healing. Today, however, there are a growing number of churches of almost every denomination rediscovering the power of prayer in healing.

Biofeedback research is revealing some of the most startling evidence of the potentiality of persons to control bodily energies and functions previously thought beyond conscious control. In biofeed-back, connections are made between specific points on a person's body and a monitoring machine so that the person sees the results of changes he effects through his own control. Researchers in this field, Dr. Barbara Brown, Dr. Joe Kamiya, Dr. Elmer Green, Dr. John Basmajian, and others are finding that a person can control to some degree any bodily function that can be monitored: heartbeat, blood pressure, gastric acid flow, brain waves, temperature of the hands, and so on. The more information received, the easier the control. Also, the longer the effort, the better the results (usually).

Other studies in this large field of research, as that on subliminal perception, show that the mind is more alert at deeper levels than the conscious mind knows.

There are a number of Christian groups, such as Christian Scientists, the Unity School of Christianity, Science of Mind, Religious Science churches, and others, who base their ministry on the power of the mind. With the exception of the Christian Scientists, most of these churches consider that almost everything that happens is caused by the mind. Human beings are free to create harmony or disharmony, health or illness.

There are today a rash of human potential courses being offered to the public based on the idea that persons can control their lives by controlling their thinking. Silva Mind Control, Earhardt Seminar

Training (EST), Creative Consciousness, and others are predicated on this philosophy, and many people have found these courses very helpful. There are self-healing courses available, teaching steps to release disharmony and create harmony through proper thinking to foster health and success in life.

Jesus' teachings and his ministry are in accord with these ideas of the power of persons to control their other lives and environment. He instructed his disciples to heal, move mountains by faith, ask whatever they would, and it would be done. His own life exemplified a power not commonly seen. The Gospels tell us he healed the sick, made the blind see, raised the dead to life, walked on water, fed five thousand with a few fish and loaves of bread, calmed a storm with a command, and other such "miracles," and told his disciples that they would do even greater things.

The church has walked around this promise of power throughout most of its history, with only occasional spiritual giants daring to appropriate it. We have hardly known what to do with the record of it. Many think that the stories of Jesus' power over the material world were due to the readiness of people to assign miraculous power to godly personalities. Others believe the power was special to Jesus, an indication of his divinity, but not available to others.

Jesus' teachings, as recorded in the Gospels, suggest a different view. He clearly talked about power over the material world as well as the spiritual, and we Christians may learn that the two are not nearly so clearly divided as we used to think. As research uncovers more and more information about the existence of energies both in and around us and the vast possibilities through the mind for its use, we are moving ever closer to doing the miraculous without resorting to magic. And as the mind moves through meditation into deeper levels of consciousness, we are tapping those resources that make it possible.

Dr. Haridas Chaudhuri, president of the California Institute of Asian Studies in San Francisco, says it this way:

> Thus, in a higher phase of meditation and yoga discipline a new kind of energy which was never known or experienced by the person before is brought into play in his life. . . . It is then he feels that the power of God is working within him. . . . And it gives a new orientation, a new direction, to the life of that individual, eventually bringing him into blissful communion with the ultimate ground of his existence. That is when the healing power reaches the height and glory of its human potential.[9]

Notes to Chapter 4

[1] Carl Simonton, "The Role of the Mind in Cancer Therapy," *The Dimensions of Healing, A Symposium* (Los Altos, Calif.: The Academy of Parapsychology and Medicine, 1972), pp. 143-144.

[2] Harold Bloomfield, "The Technology for Fulfillment," *The Western TM Reporter,* Summer, 1974 (Los Angeles: International Meditation Society), p. 7.

[3] *Ibid.,* p. 6.

[4] Robert Keith Wallace and Herbert Benson, "The Physiology of Meditation," *Scientific American,* vol. 226, no. 2 (Feb., 1972), pp. 85-90.

[5] Bloomfield, "The Technology for Fulfillment," p. 7.

[6] Jack Forem, *Transcendental Meditation* (New York: E. P. Dutton & Co., Inc., 1974), p. 56.

[7] "Mind Over Drugs," *Time,* vol. 98, no. 17 (Oct. 25, 1971), p. 51.

[8] George Leonard, "In God's Image," *Saturday Review,* vol. 2, no. 11 (Feb. 22, 1975), p. 13.

[9] Haridas Chaudhuri, "The Healing Potential of Psychosomatic Integration," *The Dimensions of Healing, A Symposium* (Los Altos, Calif.: The Academy of Parapsychology and Medicine, 1972), p. 39.

CHAPTER 5

Meditation Methods

Meditation has an ancient history. It has been a part of basic religious practices dating back to antiquity. Meditation techniques still being used have developed through the centuries in Hinduism, Buddhism, Christianity, Taoism, and others. And, in the larger cities of the United States today, many of the methods from these religions can be learned. Transcendental Meditation, a form of Hindu meditation, can be studied in most large cities at the Science of Creative Intelligence centers and on many university campuses. Yoga classes also are readily available. The disciplines of Yoga and Yoga meditation are also Hindu, and Hatha Yoga is popular in this country. Considered primarily body conditioning by the American initiate, Hatha Yoga in Hinduism is believed valuable as an aid with pranayama (proper breathing) and meditation for the harmonious development of body, mind, and spirit.

From the Buddhist tradition, the meditation system most frequently taught here is Zen Meditation, or zazen, the word for sitting meditation. Other practices being taught in the West come out of Lamaism, the religion of Tibet, another branch of Buddhism.

Delving deeply into the multitude of available meditation forms from these religions would be a time-consuming distraction from our purposes. Most of us have neither the leisure nor the motivation to make of meditation the all-consuming activity it is for the serious Hindu or Buddhist. However, it is helpful to learn some of the techniques so that our meditation periods may be efficiently beneficial for our own purposes.

Since meditation techniques of any variety borrow heavily from these ancient traditions, we need to have a healthy respect for them. Many Christians have little or no knowledge of other world religions. Fortunately, in our day, we no longer look on these great religions as "heathen," devoid of any truths of God. We are learning that all great religions are vehicles through which we can seek and find a relationship with reality, with our highest self, and with God. As Christians, we feel that we have received the highest revelation of God through Christ, but we can still appreciate the strengths of other religions, such as their meditation techniques. But unless we have some understanding of and appreciation for the source of these meditation techniques, we will be less willing to work with them. So, to gain a little clearer perspective, we will look briefly at some of the basic ideas of these religions before sampling their meditation techniques.

Hinduism, the dominant religion of India, traces its beginnings to times preceding the first sacred works, *The Four Vedas,* which were written about 1000 B.C. Hinduism teaches the existence of Brahman, the Supreme World-Soul or Spirit, who is perfect, unchanging. Brahman is the only reality and forms the inmost essence of everything, but cannot be described in human terms because all human attributes imply limitation and imperfection. Hinduism allows the worship of many gods as steps to understanding Braham, of whom they are considered an aspect. The goal of Hinduism is union with Brahman, which is bliss beyond pain or change.

The discipline through which a person achieves union with Brahman in Hinduism is called Yoga. Yoga means union or yoke, and it involves various paths of training, each leading to a higher way. At the bottom the training is purely physical, and at the top only spiritual; it is both mental and physical at the intermediate levels. The preparatory path, called Hatha Yoga, leads to higher ends, more spiritual disciplines. Meditation is a part of the Yoga disciplines at all levels.

Buddhism was begun by Gautama Buddha as a protest against

the caste system and some of the other doctrines of the Hindu religion. Buddha is a Sanskrit word meaning to be enlightened, and Gautama Siddhartha gained the name of Buddha after a long search for enlightenment using the austere Hindu Yoga practices. However, this effort did not lead to his goal, and his enlightenment came only after he had abandoned this strained approach. After his enlightenment, he taught of Four Noble Truths dealing with the recognition of desire as the cause of suffering and the elimination of it as the way to reach Nirvana, perfect freedom and peace, perfect insight. His followers try to win freedom from desire by following the Noble Eightfold Path of right belief, right aspiration, right speech, right action, right livelihood, right effort, right thought, and right meditation.

Freedom from desire does not imply, as is so often believed in the West, loss of interest, purpose, awareness. On the contrary, these attributes can become more real as the anxiety to achieve, to own, to be successful in the phenomenal world is replaced by unconcern about results. This reminds us of Jesus' teachings about taking no thought for the morrow, not being anxious, seeking God's kingdom rather than our success.

After Buddha's death, his followers separated into two groups, the Hinayana (small vehicle), which kept the simple, austere rules of discipleship, and the Mahayana (larger vehicle), which expanded the original teachings to include other buddhas and saints and their teachings.

Zen Buddhism is a Buddhist sect in the Mahayana tradition. Zen is the way of practice, as opposed to theory, and is the branch of meditative Buddhism, or zazen which is sitting meditation. Zen Buddhism has been called the way of "Mind Only," not for philosophical speculation but for intuitive awareness. It was taken to China from India in the sixth century and was greatly influenced by Taoism. In the seventh century, missionaries took it to Japan. The koan, a statement similar to a riddle, is used by the Zen student for meditation. He tries to react to this riddle with intuition rather than with logical reasoning in order to move into a higher level of understanding.

Taoism, according to tradition, was begun some 2,500 years ago in China by Lao-tse who wrote the book that has become the sacred book of the Taoist, *Tao Te Ching* (The Way and Its Power). Taoism was greatly influenced by Buddhism.

Lamaism, another branch of Buddhism, has been the major religion of Tibet and Mongolia. The unusual abilities of the lamas (monks) to control body movements usually considered involuntary have received publicity in this country.

The Easterner and the Westerner can benefit greatly from understanding each other. If we are quick to censure those of the East for willingness to contemplate while taking little action to correct social ills, we need to know that right action is basic to their religion. They can just as easily judge us for being caught up in a materialistic world, although Jesus taught that we cannot serve both God and mammon, and that it does little good to gain the world and lose our souls.

The Easterner can learn from the Westerner's impetus for action, and the Westerner can learn much from the Easterner's habit of tuning himself to inner reality, of practicing the presence of God. Our Christian religion is not diminished by acknowledgment of greatness in other religions. In fact, even a cursory study of these religions shows striking similarities to our purposes and values as Christians. Even so, it isn't necessary to accept their dogma to benefit from the techniques for meditation developed through the centuries.

All these religions greatly influenced each other, and many of the practices are similar to those of the serious Christian mystic attempting to reach a state of purification and worthiness.

Meditation techniques attempt to move a person into another state of consciousness, another way of perceiving reality different from the usual reliance on sense perception. The goal is the reality behind the symbols. Alan Watts puts it succinctly:

> Most of us think compulsively all the time; we talk to ourselves. If I talk all the time I don't hear what anyone else has to say. In exactly the same way, if I think all the time, that is to say if I talk to myself all the time, I don't have anything to think about except thoughts. Therefore, I'm living entirely in the world of symbols and I'm never in relationship with reality. I want to get in touch with reality. That's the basic reason for meditation.[1]

There are many ways to classify and organize the various techniques, but most methods, no matter how classified, purpose to still the mind of its usual activity by centering thought at one point. By focusing on only one thing, other thoughts are released, and the mind moves into a more subtle level of consciousness, eventually reaching the essence behind the symbol. Let us now look at a few samples of the various kinds of methods used for this purpose.

Breathing Techniques

Although proper breathing is used in Yoga in correlation with meditation and usually precedes it, some breathing exercises are also aids to one-pointed concentration. Pranayama, the conscious control of breathing and concentration of thought, is concerned with the taking in of Prana, considered a universal force. Prana is believed to be in the air but not identical with it; it is also in all other things. It is considered the vital element in breath and essential for health. This is the reason that the Yoga complete breath, which fills the abdomen, the diaphragm, and the lungs, is considered the standard exercise and other breathing exercises are considered variations of this. The following paragraphs include short descriptions of some of these breathing exercises which will enhance meditation.

(1) One simple breathing exercise that can be used immediately before meditation is called the Sukha Pranayama. Instructions for this are: Close the right nostril with the right thumb. Breathe out slowly, but completely, through the left nostril. Breathe in through the same nostril. Close the left nostril with the middle finger. Breathe out through the right nostril and in through the same nostril. Repeat four or five times.[2]

(2) Counting the breaths is a standard Buddhist technique for one-pointed concentration. Count the inhalations or the exhalations, not both. Your breathing will soften as this progresses. Keep your mind on your breathing, letting go of any other thoughts that pass through your consciousness. Some people prefer to count to ten and then begin again. Others prefer to count only to four. This preference is unimportant. Any method of counting the breaths can be used.[3]

(3) Observing the breath is another frequently used breathing exercise. Do not concentrate greatly on changing your breath or controlling it; do not count it. Only be aware of it, the rhythm, the space between the in and the out, the out and in. Just watch your breathing.[4]

(4) Another breathing exercise is good for relaxation to prepare the body for meditation. Stand. Spread your arms so your hands are parallel to the floor. Push your hands down hard as you exhale through your nose in three efforts. Then turn the palms of your hands

up and inhale fully and naturally. Repeat the procedure four or five times. Then sit. Continue the breathing, but hold your breath at the top of the inhalation and at the bottom of the exhalation. At both top and bottom, insert the mantra you will use in meditation. (See page 61 for a discussion of mantra.) Repeat this four or five times, then discontinue thinking of the breathing and continue thinking the mantra.[5]

An Exercise in Bare Attention

One of the simplest ways to meditate is taught by the Southern Buddhists. Sit in silence and be aware of your thoughts, states of emotion, and such in the present. Don't think about your thoughts, merely note them. Your mind is kept from wandering because when it wanders, you note this. That is in keeping with the plan, to become aware of your thoughts.[6]

Sensory Aids to One-Pointed Concentration

(1) Select some object for a point of focus, such as a ring, flower, religious symbol, or picture. A lighted candle can be used. Look at it. Keep your thoughts centered around it. When other thoughts come, let them go, and gently bring your mind back to the object. Close your eyes and visualize the object. When you have trouble visualizing, open your eyes and look again at the object. Forcing should be avoided. The goal is to center gently your thinking.[7]

(2) In the Yoga methods, pratyahara, which is sensory awareness, is often used. Select one sensory aspect of something to experience beyond the usual ways. Look at an object as though you were seeing it for the first time. Be open and receptive to receive impressions without preconceptions cluttering up the message. Use any sense of the body for this kind of experience. See a sunrise, touch a leaf, taste a new kind of tea, listen to the tick of a clock. See, hear, smell, taste, or touch something in order to tune in on only one fine point.[8]

(3) The following is a description of a visual exercise using a candle.

> Set a candle at a distance of about twenty inches in front of you. The height of the flame should be at a level with a point between your eyebrows when you are sitting up straight. Sit comfortably, but with head, neck and chest in a straight line . . .

Starting with five minutes and increasing by about five minutes a day up to one hour . . . just sit with the candle.

Don't try to do anything. Just hang out with the candleflame. Let any thoughts that enter your mind pass by like clouds in the sky. See all thoughts and sensations as tiny insects hovering around the flame. Don't try to make the flame change or to focus or to see . . . just BE with the flame. If your eyes water it is all right. If your eyes hurt, then stop.

After a period of time there will be just you and the candleflame . . . Note: You may do Japa (mantra on name of God) simultaneously if you wish.[9]

(4) An auditory exercise, called Nad Yoga, is a meditation of listening to the inner sounds. All external noises should be eliminated as much as possible. Shut your eyes. Tune in on any inner sound in your head. Find only one sound and listen. As the sound fills your consciousness, you will finally merge with that sound and hear it no longer. At that point, you will detect another sound. Tune in on the new sound and repeat the process.[10]

Mantras

Mantras are sounds that are repeated in the mind to achieve the one-pointed concentration. In the Hindu tradition there are mantras that have been used for thousands of years. The term "Japa" is used for a mantra that is a name for God.

The mantra focuses the mind on only that sound, thus it eliminates from the consciousness other preoccupations characteristic of it. Then as this sound, or mantra, is repeated, even this fades and the meditator is moved into other levels of consciousness. Some methods claim that it is better to use mantras which have no meaning attached to them, such as Sanskrit words which are given to TM initiates for mantras. They believe that attaching meaning to sounds encumbers them and makes one-pointed concentration more difficult. Others prefer meaningful mantras, particularly if the meditation is aiming for a specific result.

There are different mantras for different purposes. Some mantras are supposed to resonate within and open up your chakras (energy centers). Others are supposed to strengthen the will; others to increase compassion. There are mantras to accompany certain actions, and mantras for certain times of the day. However, most general ones in use are supposed to move a person from one stage of development to the next until the person arrives at a place where a mantra is not necessary.

There are many words for God used as mantras in various traditions, such as Krishna and Rama. However, the one considered by many persons to be the most holy sound for God's name is the OM.

To use the OM as a mantra, part the lips slightly and make the sound that comes easiest. It will sound like "Ah." Then as the sound begins to flow, close the lips slightly and the sound becomes "OO." Then, as the lips are closed, the "MM" sound is made. Some write it "AUM" for the sounds; the sounds, "AH — OO — MM," suggest that spelling. The sound should be made without forcing. It is considered by the ancients the sound of the Universal Consciousness or the universal vibration.[11]

Some other well-known mantras are:

Rama
Hari Krishna
Gate Gate Paragate
Parasamgate Bodhi Swaha (Beyond, beyond, beyond the beyond. To thee, homage!)
Om Mani Padme Hum
Om Tat Sat
Om Namah Shivaya (To Siva, I bow)[12]

The use of the rosary, beads to help the memory, in the recitation of prayers in the Roman Catholic Church is similar to the meditations using mantras.

Koans

In Zen Buddhism the student is taught to reject intellectualism, but to seek truth through a more intuitive, less strained method. Frequently used is the koan, which is an insoluble riddle supposed to propel the student who intuitively solves the riddle to a new level of truth. "There are thousands of koans and admittedly they do not make much sense to us. Nor are they supposed to. To the person who is getting near a new way of grasping the truth, however, the koan projects him over the border line and he awakens."[13]

Some examples of the koans are:

(1) Describe the sound of one hand clapping.

(2) How can a man standing on tiptoe on a mountaintop and reaching up reach even higher?

(3) How does one play the solid iron flute which is without holes?[14]

Techniques Involving the Energy Centers

Many ancient and modern teachers of meditation teach that there are seven energy centers, believed to be the repositories of energy available for use in all our efforts and, in particular, for our spiritual development. Somewhat related to the endocrine glands, they are thought of as located near the sexual organs, the spleen, the solar plexis, the heart, the throat, the brow, and the crown. They are believed to parallel somewhat the development in physical vitality, mental vitality, intuition, compassion, willpower, spiritual receptivity, and union with God.

The first three energy centers are considered as the lower chakras because their energies are thought to be primarily used in survival, sexual activity, and development of power. The other four chakras are considered the higher. As a person develops in his spiritual life, his focus is elevated to center on compassion, self-discipline, and receptivity to God.[15]

Dr. Richard Alpert believes that most people in their purposes today are at the level of development concerned with the energy from the first three chakras.

In our Western culture there has been such an investment in the models of man associated with the second and third chakras (sex and power) that we have developed strong and deeply held habits of perceiving the inner and outer universe in these terms. Though we may realize intellectually that the spiritual journey requires the transformation of energy from these preoccupations to higher centers, we find it difficult to override these strong habits which seem to be reinforced by the vibration of the culture in which we live.

Thus it seems "normal" to have certain ego needs with regard to sex and power. It is difficult for us to comprehend that what is normal for a second-chakra preoccupied person is hardly normal for a fourth-chakra person.[16]

Most teachers of meditation assume that these energy centers are involved in meditation. However, there are some exercises that purpose specifically to open these centers and move the energy upwards. Usually these are visualization exercises. The following is a compilation by this writer, but is a shortened version typical of this kind of meditation.

Visualize a bright light. See it resting at the root center of your body, creating a whirling disk of light and energy. See this ball of light move upward to your spleen center. Visualize it there as it becomes brighter and whirls in position. Let it rest there for a moment. Then see the light move on to your solar plexus center, again increasing in size and intensity. Watch it pulsate there for a period. Then see it move to your heart center, adding new power. See it whirl in position there, opening your heart center. Follow its slow journey to your throat center, enlarged and empowered there, still whirling in position. See it then move to the brow center between the eyes. See it again intensify and envelop the crown center at the top of your head. See it open these spiritual centers. See the light spread in area until it is large enough to envelop the entire body. Feel all the energy centers completely open as your body is covered with a cloud of pulsating light. Sit in the silence and feel the force of the energy. After the period of silence, begin with the crown center and allow it to close. Feel the brow center close, the throat center, the heart center, the solar plexus center, the spleen center, and the root center. Then sit in the silence knowing that you have received unlimited energy with which to pursue your purposes.

Techniques Involving Action

There are two major divisions of techniques used in the East for the achieving of pointed concentration through action. One division consists of skills performed with a total attention to mastering them. Archery, flower arrangement, aikido and karate (methods of unarmed combat), and rug weaving are examples of this. The goal is pure concentration on the task, being aware of nothing else. The other division consists of action which makes one aware of the body and its movements or focuses the attention on rhythm. The Whirling Dervish dances of the Sufi mystical tradition of Islam fall into this category, as do Hatha Yoga, T'ai Chi, and a few Western developments in sensory awareness. Also in this category would come the movement accompanying the chanting by members of the Society of Krishna Consciousness.

We will give here a Sufi movement meditation that can be done with a small group of people. Join hands in a circle. Place your feet solidly so that balance can be maintained.

Slowly lean backward, raise your face to the sky and your hands upward, and when looking as straight up as is comfortable, say in a ringing voice, "Ya Hai." Bring the body and head forward and the arms down and back until you are facing as directly downward as is comfortable. Say in the same voice "Ya Huk." Now move upward to the "Ya Hai" position and repeat.[17]

This pattern should be continued until the group has found its own rhythm. The goal is to move past the point of fatigue to total awareness of the harmony of action and sound. At the beginning, however, a group may feel that five or ten minutes is sufficient. They may keep a goal of approximately thirty minutes in mind. Anyone who needs to discontinue during the exercise may join the hands of those on either side of him and step out.

Similar Techniques from Christian Mystics

Meditation techniques being taught today are not as strange to Christianity as some may initially feel. Similar techniques have often been suggested as exercises for growth by Christian mystics throughout the history of the church. Let us look at a few of these to see the similarities.

(1) One of the examples closest to the path of action is that of the nineteenth-century French mystic and saint of the Roman Catholic Church, Therese of Lisieux. Explained in her writings, *The Little Way,* her way consisted in total concentration on her everyday household tasks to achieve perfection and harmony in the immediate as a way of relating to the total harmony of the universe.[18]

(2) An exercise using God's name as a mantra is suggested by the unknown author of *The Cloud of Unknowing,* a fourteenth-century practical guide to contemplation.

> If you want to gather all your desire into one simple word that the mind can easily retain, choose a short word rather than a long one. A one-syllable word such as "God" or "love" is best. But choose one that is meaningful to you. . . . Use it to beat upon the cloud of darkness above you and to subdue all distractions, consigning them to the *cloud of forgetting* beneath you. Should some thoughts go on annoying you demanding to know what you are doing, answer with this one word alone. If your mind begins to intellectualize over the meaning and connotations of this little word, remind yourself that its value lies in its simplicity. Do this and I assure you that these thoughts will vanish. Why? Because you have refused to develop them with arguing.[19]

(3) St. Ignatius Loyola of the sixteenth century offers the following exercise similar to the breathing techniques mentioned. Ignatius Loyola is best remembered as a Spanish leader in the Counter-Reformation of the Roman Catholic Church and as the founder of the Society of Jesus, better known as the Jesuits. "The third method of prayer is that with each breath or respiration, prayer be made mentally, saying one word of the *Our Father,* or of any other

prayer that is being recited, in such a way that only one word be said between one breath and another."[20]

This comes from *The Spiritual Exercises of St. Ignatius* which is still in use today as a guide for silent retreats in the Roman Catholic Church.

(4) An intensive attention to the presence of God is the practice most frequently suggested by the Christian mystic for achieving the one-pointed concentration necessary to carry a person to a higher spiritual state.

Bernard of Clairvaux, born near the end of the eleventh century in France, calls such listening attention to God "consideration": "Do you ask what piety is? It is leaving time for consideration. . . . What is so essential to the worship of God as the practice to which He exhorts in the Psalm, 'Be still and know that I am God.'"[21]

A similar exhortation is found in the *Imitation of Christ,* a devotional classic of the fifteenth century from a spiritual group in Holland called the Brethren of the Common Life.

> Seek a convenient time of leisure for thyself and meditate often upon God's loving-kindness.
> If thou desirest true contrition of heart, enter into thy secret chamber, and shut out the tumults of the world; as it is written, "Commune with your own heart, and in your chamber, and be still. . . ."
> Wait, wait, I say, for me; I will come and heal thee.[22]

And from the *Dark Night of the Soul,* a sixteenth-century classic by St. John of the Cross, comes the same message. During the extreme periods of spiritual dryness, which he terms the dark night of the soul, the seekers are instructed to keep their attention on God.

> What they must do is merely to leave the soul free and disencumbered and at rest from all knowledge and thought, troubling not themselves, in that state, about what they shall think or meditate upon, but contenting themselves with merely a peaceful and loving attentiveness toward God.[23]

Brother Lawrence, the seventeenth-century Carmelite monk of France, in his book on the devotional life, *The Practice of the Presence of God,* claims a similar practice. "And I make it my business only to persevere in His holy presence, wherein I keep myself by a simple attention, and a general fond regard to God, which I may call an *actual presence* of God."[24]

Henry Scougal, seventeenth-century mystic of Scotland, describes also a wordless attention to God in his book *The Life of God in the Soul of Man.*

. . . so there is a third and more sublime kind of prayer wherein the soul takes a higher flight, and having collected all its forces by long and serious meditation, it darts (If I may so speak) toward God in sighs and groans and thoughts too big for expression.[25]

Whether the one-pointed concentration is achieved through some mental technique, action, or through a concentrated attention to God, the result for which the meditator strives is the same, to touch reality behind the symbol; for the Christian, to be changed by the experience of the reality of the presence of God.

The results of meditation come slowly and imperceptibly. "The kingdom of God cometh not with observation," but it comes. Look back after six months or a year and observe the transformation of the whole being that has taken place, for it should result in a widening and purifying of the outlook, an increasingly tender and sympathetic response to the moods and needs of others, a more delicate and lovely sense of the Divine Beauty around us, a growth of what William James called the "feeling" of things, even a dawning sense of the eternal Presence of the Great Lover and Companion of all life.[26]

Notes to Chapter 5

[1] Alan Watts, *Meditation* (Millbrae, Calif.: Celestial Arts, 1974), p. 11.

[2] Richard Alpert, *Remember, Be Here Now* (San Cristobal, N. Mex.: Lama Foundation, 1971), p. 45.

[3] Justin F. Stone, *The Joys of Meditation* (Albuquerque, N.Mex.: Sun Books, 1973), p. 51.

[4] *Ibid.*, p. 51.

[5] *Ibid.*, p. 38.

[6] Richard Alpert, *Remember, Be Here Now*, p. 81.

[7] Frank J. MacHovec, *OM: A Guide to Meditation and Inner Tranquility* (New York: Peter Pauper Press, 1973), pp. 17-18.

[8] *Ibid.*, pp. 29-34.

[9] Richard Alpert, *Remember, Be Here Now*, p. 83.

[10] *Ibid.*

[11] Frank J. MacHovec, *OM,* pp. 25-27.

[12] Richard Alpert, *Remember, Be Here Now,* p. 34.

[13] John Lewis, *The Religions of the World Made Simple* (New York: Doubleday and Company, Inc., 1968), p. 49.

[14] Frank J. MacHovec, *OM,* p. 57.

[15] Elsie Sechrist, *Meditation—Gateway to Light* (Virginia Beach, Va.: Association for Research and Enlightenment Press, 1972), pp. 11-29.

[16] Richard Alpert, *Remember, Be Here Now,* p. 47.

[17] Lawrence LeShan, *How to Meditate: A Guide to Self-Discovery* (Boston: Little, Brown, and Company, 1974), pp. 98-99.

[18] Father Joseph Vann, O.F.M. ed., *Lives of Saints* (Union City, N.J.: John J. Crawley and Co., Inc., 1954), pp. 456-457.

[19] William Johnston, ed., *The Cloud of Unknowing* (Garden City: Image Books, imprint of Doubleday and Company, Inc., 1973), p. 56. Copyright © 1973 by William Johnston. Reprinted by permission of Doubleday and Company, Inc.

[20] St. Ignatius of Loyola, *The Spiritual Exercises of St. Ignatius* (New York: Catholic Book Publishing Co., 1956), p. 123.

[21] Douglas V. Steere, ed., *Bernard of Clairvaux* (Nashville, Tenn.: The Upper Room, 1961), p. 7.

[22] Douglas V. Steere, ed., *The Imitation of Christ* (Nashville, Tenn.: The Upper Room, 1950), pp. 23-24.

[23] E. Allison Peers, trans. and ed., *Dark Night of the Soul* (Garden City, N.Y.: Image Books, imprint of Doubleday and Company, Inc., 1959), p. 71.

[24] Brother Lawrence, *The Practice of the Presence of God* (Old Tappan, N.J.: Fleming H. Revell Company, 1958), p. 37.

[25] Thomas S. Kepler, ed., *The Life of God in the Soul of Man* (Nashville: The Upper Room, 1962), p. 13.

[26] Clara M. Codd, *Meditation, Its Practice and Results* (Wheaton, Ill. Theosophical Publishing House, 1971), p. 52.

CHAPTER 6

Beginning Individual Meditation

To achieve results, reading about meditation must eventually give way to practicing it. The theory will never make any difference unless it is used.

There are very few necessities for beginning. A quiet place, a half hour of undisturbed time, and the willingness to begin seriously are the only basic requirements.

The best time of day for meditation for each person is that which fits most comfortably into his or her normal routine. For many people there is little extra time available in their regular schedule, and additional time must be found. One way to add an extra half hour to the day is by rising thirty minutes earlier in the morning. Although this is difficult for people who already have trouble getting started each day, it shows serious intent and gives good impetus to a new practice. Since meditation results in extra energy, the thirty minutes of missed sleep will probably not be noticed, but the problem can also be remedied by retiring earlier in the evening. Slow morning starters will discover to their delight that after meditation, the morning moves with surprising efficiency. Although meditating in the morning is for many people an exhilarating way to begin the day, other available times can be equally valuable. If your schedule permits any flexibility, experimenting with different times of the day is a good idea. Persons will find that at some times of the day they move more easily into the meditative state than at others. Anytime except within two hours after eating and before retiring for sleep is satisfactory. After meals the body is engaged in digestive processes which interfere with meditation, and near bedtime the additional energy following meditation is not always conducive to sleep.

If possible, the same time and place each day should be used. Habits formed by such regularity facilitate meditation. However, it is better to meditate daily even if you have to change time and place.

Meditating twice a day, once early and once late, is advantageous, but once a day is also a satisfactory beginning. It is not suggested that persons just beginning meditation practice it more frequently than twice a day. Later, after they have progressed in the practice, they may want to join in meditation conferences, retreats, and such. At such gatherings, under proper direction, longer and more frequent meditation periods can be enjoyed with great benefit. However, at first, one or two periods of fifteen to twenty minutes a day is all that is necessary.

For Christians who are beginning meditation as a plan for spiritual growth, the meditation period should be incorporated into a devotional framework. Many Americans practicing or learning Transcendental Meditation consider it primarily an exercise for physical relaxation and well-being, and it does contribute to this. For the Christian, however, spiritual purposes should be paramount. As we relate our lives more closely to our deeper selves, that part of us already linked to God, we are enabled to move nearer the ideal of Christlikeness.

If one already has a practice of daily devotions, meditation can easily fit into such a period. For many without such a daily habit, this will be a new experience. The following suggested format for a devotional period is offered. Naturally it should be varied in any way that is helpful.

1. *Prayer.* Begin with prayer. This can be a simple one-sentence turning of ourselves to God; the length is not important. Words from Psalm 19, "Let the words of my mouth and the meditation of my heart be acceptable in thy sight, O Lord, my rock and my redeemer," can be used as a prayer for beginning. Thoughtfully praying the Lord's Prayer is an excellent way to begin the devotional period.

2. *Inspirational Reading.* Reading inspirational material before meditation elevates the thinking and helps create the proper atmosphere. The Bible, of course, is the Christian's basic book for inspiration. Part Two of this book has selections that may be used for this purpose. Listed in the back of the book are some devotional classics and current inspirational books. Also available are daily devotional booklets, such as *The Secret Place, The Upper Room, Daily Word,* and the *Christian Science Quarterly,* which give short devotional messages or suggestions for Bible study for each day of the month. Any such reading can be beneficial.

If a person has limited time for the meditation period, this reading can be deferred until another time of the day. Inspirational reading is good bedtime material. It is conducive to peaceful, relaxed feelings which are conducive to sleep. Books relating Christianity to life serve both to inspire and reassure us, and there are many excellent books available.

3. *The Meditation Period.* Sit in a comfortable chair with a fairly straight back. Some teachers specify that the spine be very straight and the feet firmly placed on the floor. But this is tiring to persons not used to such rigid posture, and it is better to be relaxed and comfortable so that the body can be forgotten.

Start the meditation period by breathing deeply several times and exhaling slowly. The breathing exercise given in Chapter Five to prepare for meditation is excellent and can be used for relaxing the body.

Move now into the period of silence using whatever meditation technique you choose, and stay in the silence for fifteen or twenty minutes. Take several minutes to come out of the meditation gradually.

To select a meditation technique, review the various methods given in the previous chapter. A simple method easy for beginning is the less structured technique given in Chapter One. Later, try experimenting with a mantra, a visual technique, and the breathing exercises. Over a period of weeks, try all the techniques given, if you like. You will find some more effective for you than others. Note the ones that are best for you. These techniques can be made more meaningful to Christians by varying them, using Christian terms and symbols. Some examples of how this can be done follow:

   a. A Breathing Technique. Breathe deeply, hold the inhalation at the top, and mentally repeat the words, "Lo, I am with you always." Breathe out slowly. Repeat. Continue for fifteen to twenty minutes. The breathing will soften and slow down gradually. You will notice it less. This is as it should be. The words may also fade. You may find yourself using only one word of the phrase, such as "always." Don't be concerned if this happens, for it produces a better one-pointed focus. If you become aware that you are not following the plan, gently return your thoughts to the phrase or the word and continue.

b. A Visual Technique. Choose an object with religious meaning for you, such as a cross, a picture of Jesus, the Bible, a candle, or anything else. Place the object in front of you positioned so that you can look at it. Begin the meditation by centering your attention on the object. When your thoughts stray, bring your mind back to the object. Gradually let the thinking fade and just see the object. Shut your eyes and visualize the object. When this becomes difficult, open your eyes and look again at the object. Shut your eyes and again try to visualize the object. Continue for fifteen to twenty minutes.

c. A Mantra. Choose a word that has significance for you and use this word as a mantra. Mentally repeat the word you have chosen. If the word gradually fades or changes, do not be concerned. If you become conscious of other thoughts, bring your mind back to the mantra. Do not be concerned with the other thoughts that float by; think of them as unimportant, and continue thinking the mantra without great effort. The following words can be used as mantras, and you can think of others:

> GOD
> HEAVENLY FATHER
> OUR FATHER
> FATHER
> HOLY SPIRIT
> HOLY
> LOVE
> O LORD, OUR LORD
> I AM
> JESUS CHRIST SAVIOR

Phrases can also be used, though for one-pointed concentration, shorter phrases are better than longer ones. A phrase used by Greek

Orthodox Christian mystics is "Lord Jesus Christ, have mercy on me." [1]

d. A Wordless Attention to God's Presence. This plan, frequently described in the writings of Christian mystics, is more difficult than a simple meditation technique. A person who has had some experience with meditation may attempt it. Sit in the silence and be aware of God's presence. Sometimes this state of awareness can be more easily reached by first using a phrase, such as "God is here," as a mantra until the words fade and the awareness exists without words.

e. Guided Meditation. Sometimes it is helpful to have an audible guide for meditation. Part Three of this book is a section of guided meditations. They are offered for group use, but individuals can use them by taping them. It is also quite easy for a person to work up his own meditation routine to tape for use during the devotional period. This tape could include a prayer, an inspirational quotation, such as a section from the Bible, fifteen minutes of silence or a guided meditation, and a closing prayer. The fourth guided meditation in Part Three is planned for taping for individual use. Also, the visualization exercise for opening the energy centers given in Chapter Five could be taped.

When taping a meditation, the reader should read the words slowly and softly, with appropriate pauses, and in a manner that will contribute to the quieting of the mind.

After the meditator has found a technique effective for him or her, he or she should continue meditating with it for at least a week or two. Habits are formed that contribute to the ease of moving into the meditative state, and the more a technique is used, the more effective it usually becomes. After sufficient experimentation, the best method for each person will most likely become obvious. At that time, the meditator should discontinue the experimentation and use this method for as long as it is helpful.

Often more dramatic differences between being in and out of the meditative state are noticed when a person first begins meditation. As he continues to meditate, the difference seems to diminish. A person should not become discouraged at this, thinking that he is not meditating correctly. As a person's system becomes accustomed to the meditative state, the experience of moving into it is more delicate and less dramatic.

Each day's meditation should not be critically analyzed. More is happening to the meditator than he is aware of at a coarser level of consciousness. He should meditate and accept whatever happens in the day's meditation without concern. Results should be looked for in the life of the meditator. It is there that change can be observed.

4. *Intercessory Prayer*. It is believed that meditation builds energies that can contribute to the healing and helping of others. The meditation period may be followed with prayer for the healing and helping of those who need it. "May Thy will be done in the lives of these people" is a phrase that might be used before reading a list of the names of persons in need of such help. The meditators should try mentally to attune themselves to each person as the name is read.

5. *Closing Prayer*. The devotional period should both begin and end with prayer. An example of an appropriate prayer for ending the devotional time and beginning the active portion of the day is "Not my will but thine be done in me and through me today, Heavenly Father." We begin by turning our thoughts to God. We move into meditation, relating our lives at deeper levels to God, and we close by again dedicating our activities to God. This rounds out the devotional period.

As the meditation period is most effective for Christian growth when incorporated into a devotional framework, so the devotional period is most effective incorporated into a total life effort. We are not primarily concerned with either meditation or a devotional period. We are concerned with the Christian life. For a Christian to make progress in his personal efforts for growth, he should have some goals toward which he moves. The following disciplines are offered to be used in any way that may contribute to the setting of goals for Christian growth. A person might use them by choosing to follow one for a specified period of time. Eventually all the disciplines listed below should become natural to the Christian, for they are all basic to the Christian way of life.

Disciplines

(1) Begin a practice of honest self-examination. It is difficult for us to see ourselves honestly, and it takes some courage to try. But Jesus promised that the truth will make us free. Self-examination has always been a part of Christian discipline. Although there is a

tendency for some to condemn themselves too readily, others defend every action or thought, explaining it away, so that they never face their weaknesses. The best practice is neither to condemn nor defend, but to stand as an observer and just notice our actions, words, and thoughts. Jesus never asked anyone to wallow in self-condemnation; he merely told people to go and sin no more. He was more interested in their future actions than those already past. We need to know where we are so that we can begin to move in the direction we should go.

(2) Ask in daily prayer that any negative feelings be removed from you. If you have faced yourself honestly by self-examination, you know that you have emotions and thoughts that are negative, hostilities, anger, anxieties, fears, and others. In prayer, consciously turn these over to God. The Christian is told to live free of anxiety, to love all people, to live a life of faith, hope, and compassion. Many habits of negative thinking will begin leaving us as we practice meditation, but this process can be buttressed through consciously asking that negativism be replaced with faith, hope, and love.

(3) Begin the practice of directing your thinking. As a person practices meditation, he or she sees that thoughts can truly be directed. This is not the same thing as repressing those things we do not wish to face. The proper way to replace negative thoughts with positive ones is to visualize a positive result instead of a negative one. We are constantly imagining things, future events. If we are worrying about someone we love, we are probably visualizing all the things we fear. Instead, we must visualize positive results. We are learning that thoughts have more power than we ever knew, and we must use this positive force wisely. Our thoughts then become a source of strength to the person in trouble. And we remain without anxiety, knowing that the Father who knows if a sparrow falls to the ground has us all in his care. This is the life of faith the Christian is called to live.

(4) Look for ways the basic Christian commandment, the law of love can be lived. When we begin looking for ways to live this law, we see opportunities everywhere. We may see that we can become more understanding of members of our own families. We may see ways to express helpfulness and love on our jobs or in our neighborhoods. Acts of love do not have to be large to be important. Living the law of love can gradually become natural to our living as it was with Jesus, expressing compassion in every relationship, every contact with another person, even in every thought.

(5) Begin the practice of the presence of God. Following the example of many Christian mystics, try to realize as constantly as possible during the day that God is with you, and you are in his presence. Some find that praying short prayers all during the day helps keep God's presence in mind. Dr. Frank Laubach and Brother Lawrence both reported keeping a conversation with God going all during their day. Both claimed that this practice produced efficiency in their tasks and peace and joy in their hearts.

(6) Begin choosing God's will over your own desires as far as you can discern God's will. The goal toward which the Christian moves is finding God's kingdom within, becoming the new person in Jesus Christ, finding his or her life by losing it. All these statements imply that God and his kingdom must become central to our lives, and concern for our own egos must lose its centrality. If all our time is seen as God's time; if all our material goods are considered God's; if all our loved ones are thought of as belonging not to us but to God, then life becomes a stewardship. We see everything in a different perspective.

(7) Begin the habit of expressing happiness. Often less than happy modes of expression are primarily bad habits. Meditation should contribute to a feeling of happiness, and as we try to live the law of love, to live without anxiety or hostility, we should begin to feel joyous. Jesus spoke at length about the state of being happy or blessed. Let us begin to spread, by our own expression of it, that joy that is growing inside us.

As a person practices these disciplines, others that can be followed will occur to him or her. Progress is facilitated by having definite goals toward which to move.

As Christians, we are called to live by a high standard. Two thousand years ago Jesus gave us a new model. Through our devotional life, meditation, and daily living we seek to move into deeper relationship with ourselves, God, and our fellow human beings. As we pattern ourselves after Jesus Christ, we tune our lives on all levels of consciousness to God, who is Love, that we may become God-centered people, and our every action and thought become an expression of his love. That is the Christlike way for which we strive.

Notes to Chapter 6

Richard Alpert, *Remember, Be Here Now* (San Cristobal, N. Mex.: Lama Foundation, 1971), p. 35.

CHAPTER 7

Forming
a Meditation Group
in the
Local Church

If you have read through to this chapter and have started meditating daily, you may be enthusiastic about meditation. You may not, however, feel any need for a meditation group, particularly if you are getting personal satisfaction and results from your own meditation period.

There are a number of reasons for encouraging the formation of a group within the church. For people already meditating, a group allows opportunity for sharing results, encouragement, and meditation. Group meditation can carry a person to new heights not yet experienced alone. Frequently meditators joining a group are surprised at the unity, power, exhilaration, and purposefulness generated in group meditation. It is uplifting to come together for spiritual purposes, as in meditation.

Another reason for forming a group in the church is to introduce meditation to those who either are or might become interested in learning this technique for Christian growth.

Getting an initial group together may be difficult unless interest in meditation has already been created in the community through Transcendental Meditation or some other organization. Since churches often have difficulty creating interest in new patterns of worship and devotion, the first step necessary may be to create interest in meditation as such before any kind of group can be formed. If there is a prayer group in the church, this would be a natural place to introduce meditation.

But let us consider possible ways of introducing meditation in a church where little is known about it. If there is a practicing meditator among the membership who is sufficiently vocal to share his knowledge and interest, he could serve as a speaker for this purpose. If there is a Transcendental Meditation organization in the community, speakers can be obtained there. Speakers from other groups teaching meditation are also sometimes available, but care should be used in the selection of speakers. They should present a method of meditation compatible to Christianity and one that is not too complicated or discouraging for beginners to attempt with success.

Interest can also be fostered through book reviews. Many churches regularly issue bulletins or newspapers, some of which include reviews of books relevant to the Christian community. Such space could be used for reviewing this book or others on meditation. Often book reviews are program features of women's groups, men's groups, church school classes, and others.

Official boards of the church are other logical places to begin. Most churches plan classes and events through their boards. A class to introduce or teach meditation could be initiated at this level if enough interest can be created among the board members. Special events on the church calendar, such as annual retreats, family nights at the church, spiritual emphasis meetings, and others, lend themselves well to the introduction of meditation.

Interest can be created by the enthusiasm of only one person, and the simplest way to begin would be for such a person to invite several interested people together to discuss forming a group for the purpose of learning to meditate.

When announcing the opportunity for a meditation group in the church, the plan should be clearly stated. It may be easier to interest people in a short-term class for eight to ten weeks rather than an ongoing class about something that is new to them. After the learning sessions are completed, there will probably be many who would like to continue meeting regularly as a meditation group.

Any number of persons can constitute a group. There is no need for Madison Avenue promotion for a good beginning. Small groups can be very meaningful. As the members experience the value of their efforts together, their enthusiasm will naturally spread, and the group will probably grow.

If the efforts to introduce meditation are highly successful, more than one group may be launched. Smaller groups are more effective for learning and sharing, and large numbers could be advantageously divided into groups of from nine to fifteen or so. Naturally, the church should be adaptable to whatever resources they have. If there is a teacher available, it might be preferable to meet as a larger group while the beginning lessons are learned. After that, a division into smaller groups could be made.

Membership in ongoing groups will most likely follow a common pattern of decline and growth. The decline usually comes in the first month or two. Some who thought they wanted such a group will find that they are not yet ready for such a discipline. Members who continue, conversely, will find a growing appreciation for group meditation and for the growth they see in their own lives and in the lives of others in the group. They will feel a supportive closeness from the group and an extension of their understanding and practice of Christianity. Their interest will bring others, and the group may increase to the size chosen for a limit.

Once a core of people are willing to meet regularly, there are a number of things that need to be planned. The following is a list of basic questions to be considered.

1. How frequently will the group meet?
2. When will the meetings be held?
3. How long will the meetings last?
4. Where will the group meet?
5. What plan will be used for learning to meditate?
6. What leadership will be used?
7. What plan for Christian growth will be used after the meditation techniques are learned? (This question is relevant only to the group that has chosen to be an ongoing group.)
8. Anything else?

Careful consideration should be given to each of these questions, even though they seem quite routine.

1. How frequently will the group meet? Once a week is about right. It is often enough and definitely not too often. A weekly

meeting provides time, a necessary factor for the hard effort needed to achieve the group's high purpose, learning meditation for Christian growth. A weekly meeting also builds cohesiveness in the group and allows for occasional absences without disturbing the stability of the group or weakening the commitment of the participant. If the members find that once a week is too frequent, they should try to come as near that standard as possible. Any plan that allows for regularity can be used, either during the learning sessions or later, just so the sessions are frequent enough that continuity is not lost. Meetings less frequent than once a month are probably not helpful except as a follow-up to the learning sessions or as a check on whether a person has correctly learned and is properly following the techniques.

2. When will the meetings be held? A day and time should be chosen agreeable to as many of the prospective participants as possible.

3. How long will the meetings last? An hour and a half to two hours is excellent for a weekly meeting. A group should not try to get by with less than an hour if it is to include personal sharing and the like. An hour and a half allows for several avenues of development to take place. There is time for reading, discussion, prayer, the meditation silence, and prayers for healing. There is no feeling of being rushed, and there is time for flexibility. An hour can also be used effectively if the group is firm about starting on time and follows a format with less variation. For business people who choose to use a lunch hour, such tightening will be essential, but this is better than meeting less frequently.

For groups meeting only once or twice a month, a two-hour allotment would be wiser. Two hours allow more time for reading, discussion, and fellowship with the same time for meditation. Since the members will see each other less often, it is important that enough time be allowed for them to get to know each other. Persons will benefit more from the meetings if they are comfortable with the other people and free to be themselves.

4. Where will the group meet? The meetings ideally should be held at the same place and time each session. This allows for quickly moving into the format of the meetings without adjusting to physical

changes. However, this should not be considered a rigid standard by any means. Any room that is comfortable and free from noise and interruptions can be used. A home or the church serves equally well as long as these requirements are met. Taking a nearby phone off the hook for this period eliminates one possibility for disruption.

5. What plan will be used for learning to meditate? Meditation techniques can be learned either from a teacher or from a book. If a qualified teacher is available, there is a definite advantage to personal instruction. However, it is also possible to learn to meditate from instructions given in books. This book is planned as a manual for beginning instruction, and steps for using it as such are given later in this chapter. Even if a teacher is found, a book is a good resource.

6. What leadership will be used? It is expedient for someone to be designated as leader at each meeting. If a teacher is secured, he or she will, of course, assume leadership at the start and for the first weeks after the basic techniques are learned. If the group continues after the learning sessions are over, there is no reason for the same person to lead each session. Each person brings his or her own uniqueness to the group, and the sessions will be richer for rotating the leadership. Some groups rotate leaders on a regular basis, such as every four meetings. Others are guided by the book being used as a resource, changing leaders at natural divisions of the material.

7. What plan for Christian growth will be used after the meditation techniques are learned? If the group is meeting for a limited number of weeks, this question can be ignored until or unless it becomes an ongoing group. For groups planning to continue, this is an important question.

The books of the New Testament can be used as a guide for Christian growth, particularly the teachings of Jesus as they apply to daily living. Care should be taken that the study of the Bible does not become just a literary or historical study, which, though valuable in itself, is not the purpose of this group. One of the most valuable approaches to Bible study, which would fit the purposes of a meditation group, is the consideration of what the Bible is saying to people today. It has been traditional throughout church history that the Bible speaks its truth to each generation.

There are many good books and new ones being published

constantly that can serve effectively as the basis for the work of this group. An excellent example of such books is the Search for God series of study books in two volumes published by the Association for Research and Enlightenment (ARE), Virginia Beach, Virginia. Although these books are planned for the ARE study groups, they can be purchased and used by any group. This series discusses precepts basic to Christian living and provides a plan for the group to follow leading to Christian growth. An accompanying handbook is also available. Other books for this purpose are listed in the back of this book.

Parts Two and Three of this book provide material that may be used during the meetings after the mechanics of meditation have been learned. Part Two is a section discussing various facets of Christian growth. Selections from this part can be read during the discussion period to stimulate an exchange of ideas about Christian growth and to set an atmosphere for the meditation period.

Part Three is a collection of guided meditations that may be used occasionally during the meditation silence. It is not suggested that every meditation be guided. These few are provided to serve as introductory experiences with guided meditation, but they should be interspersed with other techniques during the learning sessions and following. A group might choose to have every fourth meeting one in which they use a guided meditation. By trying a variety of techniques, the ones most helpful will stand out.

After the techniques are learned, the group may choose not to follow any one book as a guide. They may prefer instead to choose areas of Christian growth to emphasize. There are many possible goals for growth that could be featured, such as loving your enemies, loving your neighbor as yourself, loving yourself properly, loving God with all your heart, soul, and mind, seeking first the kingdom of God and his righteousness, and the like. Material can be found concerning these topics from various sources, including Part Two of this book.

8. Anything else? The group should consider, in addition to the goal of Christian growth, becoming an agency for healing for those who need it. This suggestion could be deferred until the chapter on healing energies is read and discussed, but this is a natural function of a meditation group. Many teachers believe that healing energies are generated in greater force in group meditation than in individual

meditation. The group should eventually discuss the possibility of using the period immediately following meditation to send this healing energy to those who need it through thought and prayer.

Some ground rules should be made at the planning stage about whether coffee, dessert, and the like will be served at the meetings. Dispensing with such practices allows the time to be used wholly for its serious purposes. Superfluous activities are definitely not suggested for groups meeting for only an hour each week. For groups meeting less frequently and for a two-hour period, refreshments may be helpful in creating fellowship. If refreshments are included, some simple plan should be adopted that minimizes its importance. Any eating should, of course, follow the meditation period rather than precede it.

It is important in meditation groups to start on time. It is easy to form the habit of promptness at the beginning, but hard if it becomes habitual to begin the meetings late. A disciplined approach to living is one of the goals toward which the group should be working, and this is one small discipline that can be observed at the meetings.

Also, groups are better if all members participate. Those who have a tendency to talk too much should remind themselves that there is only a certain share of center stage that rightfully belongs to them. Conversely, those who are reticent must remind themselves that they will make faster progress if they take part. Also, they have an obligation to contribute to the discussion in return for what others have given them. Ideas they may feel unimportant, if expressed, may be helpful to someone else. The person leading should be alert and should tactfully guide the group toward a balanced participation.

Finally, opportunities for growth should be discussed primarily in terms of principles rather than as personal problems. This is not to exclude personal sharing, for this is a valuable part of the interaction of the group. Care must be exerted, however, that the meetings aim consistently at their purpose, Christian growth, and avoid becoming social occasions or therapy groups.

The following format is suggested to structure the meetings. Changes should be made as the group desires and as the group changes from a class to learn technique to an ongoing meditation group.

Format for Meditation Meetings

1. Informal sharing

2. Opening prayer or affirmation
3. Instruction or reading for instruction or inspiration
4. The Lord's Prayer prayed in unison
5. Meditation—The period of silence should be approximately fifteen minutes. A variety of techniques can be tried by the group over the weeks, including the guided meditations in Part Three of this book.
6. Prayers for healing—A list of names may be kept by the group, updated each week, or each person can name weekly those he wishes to include. The statement "May God's healing energies flow through us for the healing and helping of these people" or some such short prayer can precede the reading of the names.
7. Closing—Group recitation of the Twenty-third Psalm.
8. Discussion—During this period, any subject that anyone wishes to discuss can be discussed; the techniques being used, the experiences of meditation during the week, and so on.
9. Assignment of a discipline—It is an excellent plan for the group to choose a Christian discipline to follow between meetings. Success or difficulties with this discipline can be discussed at each meeting, and another discipline chosen. Suggestions for this are given both in the previous chapter and later in this one. Other disciplines will occur to members of the group as they work on these.

How to Use This Book as an Instruction Manual

1. To organize the group, the questions listed and discussed previously can be used to guide necessary decisions.
2. Each member of the group should read Chapter One and begin meditating daily, using the simple suggestion for meditation in that chapter. Later techniques suggested in Chapter Six can be substituted for this first method. The progress made in the group depends on the effort each individual is making in his or her own daily meditations. To meditate only when the group comes together is limiting. The group meetings may have meaning for those in it who do not meditate regularly, but they will not experience the progress possible nor contribute effectively unless they meditate daily.
3. Begin the instruction sessions by reading and discussing Chapter One, "Meditation: What Is It?" This can be read at home prior to the meeting, or it can be read aloud at the meeting. Either way is a satisfactory method of assimilating the material for discussion.

4. For the first meetings, follow the format given, and during the period of quiet, use the simple exercise in meditation given in the first chapter.

5. Continue session by session the discussion of the material in the book by chapters. Through Chapter Four, use the same plan for meditation. If the group is to be an ongoing group, no hurry need be made. The group can move at the pace that is comfortable and instructive. If the class is scheduled for a limited number of weeks, the material should be divided into sections so that all the material can be adequately covered within the time limit. Reading the assigned chapter prior to the session saves time, and the meeting time can be used for discussion and assimilating the material. A ten-week course would allow one week each for most of the chapters plus two for those that might need additional time, possibly mysticism and method.

6. When Chapter Five, "Meditation Methods," is reached, a change in the meditation technique may be made. Different techniques should be tried each time. For instance, one week a mantra might be used as the method. Another week a visual aid, such as a candle, could be used. Guided meditations as occasional variations should also be tried. The purpose is to learn about a variety of techniques by experiencing them. After a number of techniques are learned and each person has time to study all the ones given, the quiet period can be left without suggestion or guidance to the individual. As a person practices meditation, he will find the most natural way to move into the silence. This will vary from person to person.

7. Continue reading through the book, including the last chapter of the first part, "Some Questions and Answers." The leader each week should choose the meditation method to be used until enough variety has been experienced.

By the time all this is completed, the group will have learned about as much as this book intends to teach them. But the group should be firmly launched on an adventure of the spirit that can lead on and on to more growth in the Way of Christ.

Suggested Disciplines

These are offered as a small sampling of what is possible. Others will occur to members as different materials are studied. Each member should select a discipline to apply consciously to his or her daily life which will lead more directly to his or her purpose of growing as a Christian.

1. During daily meditation, use a visualization meditation as a solution to some problem in your life. Note the visualization technique in the section on guided meditations for an example of this. Visualize a successful and happy outcome in harmony with your Christian ideals.

2. Practice seeing God's spirit in the people you come in contact with daily. Look for the good, the pure, the loving nature in all people.

3. Write down hunches, dreams, ideas, that intuitively come to you offering Christian guidance to your living.

4. Write down a spiritual goal you wish to achieve in the next six months. Rewirte it each week, refining the wording and changing the direction as insights come to you.

5. Change any daily habit that does not contribute to health and happiness. Substitute a good habit for a poor one that you want to change. For instance, short periods of exercise can be substituted for short periods of eating if overeating is a problem.

6. Cultivate the habit of expressing appreciation to someone each day for something they have done for you or for anyone or anything. When we look for it, we see the support out lives are receiving on every front. Let us begin to show gratitude.

CHAPTER 8

Some Questions and Answers

Answers are given here to questions frequently asked when meditation is presented to church groups.

1. *Did Jesus meditate?*

Nothing is mentioned in the New Testament about Jesus practicing a formal system of meditation. However, he often withdrew for periods alone, as he did the forty days in the wilderness. He obviously lived in awareness of God's presence, and his final decisions showed him following, even unto death, God's will rather than his own. He unquestionably had some way of realizing God's presence and will, of achieving a heightened spiritual receptivity. Thomas Kelly, in his classic book of the devotional life, *A Testament of Devotion,* calls it "inward orientation," "inward worship and listening," "This practice is the heart of religion. It is the secret, I am persuaded, of the inner life of the Master of Galilee."[1] It is meditation in the highest sense, an awareness of God's presence permeating all levels of consciousness.

2. *Why is prayer not sufficient? Why add meditation to it?*

The meditative state we are concerned with is another level of consciousness, one that research shows to be different from other wakeful or sleep states, as discussed in Chapter One. Prayer is directing thoughts toward God in a normal, wakeful state. It is beneficial for a person to begin his devotional period with prayer, energy flowing outward, and then to move into a receptive meditative state. This gives a completeness to the devotional life. We turn with an outpouring of ourselves toward God, then wait in the silence to receive.

3. *Can a person receive specific answers to prayers or guidance about problems in meditation?*

Yes, this is possible, and a person should pay attention to insights and intuitive answers that come to him or her through meditation. However, meditation should not be considered as some kind of magic resource. As persons are responsible for their own decisions, they must face facts honestly and not look for "signs" that an outside answer has been given. By meditating daily, a person grows in the knowledge of who he or she is and what his or her real purposes are. Then, when problems arise, he or she knows better how to deal with them.

4. *If meditation contributes to healing, couldn't we, by meditating, be tampering with God's will? How do we know that illness isn't God-given for spiritual growth?*

There is nothing in Jesus' teachings suggesting that illness is ever given by God. Jesus spent much of his time healing, and we do not hesitate today to go to doctors for help. There is only one story in the New Testament showing a purpose of God through a physical problem. This is the story of the boy born blind. In John 9:1 it is reported that Jesus was asked if the boy were born blind because of his own sin or that of his parents. Jesus replied that it was neither, but "that the works of God might be made manifest in him" (v. 3). Although this story raises philosophical questions, God is shown even here to be favoring healing.

Any challenge or hardship faced courageously can add to spiritual stature, and illness is therefore sometimes the stimulus for such a period of inner growth. But we should never confuse illness with God's will. His will is shown repeatedly in the New Testament to be for health and wholeness.

5. *Is meditation really a "Christian" activity? If it can be such a great help to a Christian, why do some Christians feel so hesitant about it?*

There are a number of reasons. First, our churches today are geared toward activity. Anything that requires us to sit still and do nothing is suspect. With so much to be done, we feel guilty, afraid we are wasting time. And there is the fear of the unknown which is a common experience. Also, many of the meditation techniques come out of Hinduism, Buddhism, and other religions, and this makes some Christians uncomfortable. We do not appreciate the quality of these religions because we know so little about them. It is only as we see similarities between their goals and ideals and ours that we realize God has made himself known to all people, and we are all truly his children. Then we can share our revelation with them and receive from theirs, seeing perhaps how the revelation of God through Christ can be the fulfillment of their revelation as it was that of the Jewish heritage for the Christian.

Also, a majority of church members know little about the rich mystic strain in church history, although they are the beneficiaries of it. Many of the meditation techniques used today are similar or identical to the disciplines practiced by mystics throughout church history. Moving into silence to become aware of God's presence cannot be considered unchristian.

6. *Is there any danger in meditation?*

In the devotional framework of God's presence, meditation for the Christian can be only beneficial. Intense concentration techniques taught by some black magic, witchcraft, satanic, and other occult groups can be extremely dangerous. This is not meditation, and no Christian should have anything to do with it. Meditation is a gentle centering down and has been found through research to be extremely physically beneficial.

7. *Can meditation become an escape from life?*

Yes, meditation does enable a person to escape for a period. It is a positive, renewing escape which permits the person to return to his or her normal activities better able to cope with them. All people need means of escaping periodically from the stresses and tensions of their daily lives. Recreational activities do this also. Those who seek this escape through alcohol, drugs, and other unhealthy means do not return to life better able to handle its problems.

8. *Is there anything done in meditation that can't be done faster with biofeedback?*

Meditation and biofeedback activities are not alike at all except that both can produce alpha waves in the brain and physiological changes in the body. Biofeedback is used to monitor physical reactions for the purpose of changing them. Meditation is not solely for the purpose of generating alpha waves or even for changing the physiology of a person, although physiological changes do take place. As a Christian meditates, he or she is tuning himself or herself to universal purposes and energies for growth in Christlikeness. This can't be monitored with a machine.

9. *Can psychic abilities be developed through meditation?*

People occasionally report psychic experiences or abilities after they have started meditating. In the East, students of meditation are told that if they ignore such development, it will go away. The development of psychic abilities does not necessarily parallel spiritual progress, and the latter is the primary goal. To become overly interested in developing psychic skills can be a distraction from the more important goal.

10. *But couldn't psychic abilities be a great benefit to humankind?*

This is true, as it is of any power. When psychic abilities are developed in a spiritually mature person, great good can come from the combination. Just as atomic power can be used for the benefit or destruction of persons, so it is with all power, psychic powers included. Psychic powers are neither good nor bad in themselves. They can contribute to either depending on how they are used. It is therefore wise to develop spiritual maturity as a first objective.

11. *Would it be better to take Transcendental Meditation instruction than to try to learn to meditate any other way?*

This is an easy method to learn, and TM centers are located in most large cities. Since there is a fee, it is difficult for some to finance, and there are other ways to learn. A good method can be discovered by trying the various techniques given in this book. Any technique that enables a person to move into a meditative state is an acceptable tool, but for the Christian this should only be a beginning. By following the suggestions in Chapter Six, meditation can be incorporated into a larger plan for Christian growth. Even with TM instruction, a Christian will get maximum help from meditation by enclosing it in a devotional framework.

12. *Meditation seems to help some people more than others. Is there only a certain type who benefit from meditation?*

Some people have a more naturally contemplative temperament than others. This doesn't mean that there is anyone who cannot benefit from meditation. Frequently people do not reap the results possible from meditation because they do not make it a regular daily practice. They do not try hard enough. Others try too hard, watching too closely for dramatic results. The more active, less introspective types can benefit greatly from meditation, but they may have a harder time applying the principles necessary for results.

13. *If a person is just beginning meditation, how long will he or she need to meditate before he or she experiences Cosmic Consciousness?*

The ultimate experience called Cosmic Consciousness can come anytime, or it may never come. It cannot be programmed. We are told to ask, seek, and knock, but we must cultivate an attitude of acceptance of growth as it comes, while we make constant and consistent effort. The Zen Buddhists have a saying, "Do not push the river." [2] We flow with the rhythm of our lives as we move in the right direction. Cosmic Consciousness comes as a gift, not as our achievement. It is not the only state of joy that results from meditation, and these lesser states of joy can be experienced soon after learning meditation. It is more important, however, to use our meditation as a means of growth. Thomas Kelly says, "States of consciousness are fluctuating. The vision fades. But holy and listening and alert obedience remains, as the core and kernel of a God-intoxicated life, as the abiding pattern of sober, workaday living." [3]

14. *Can children learn to meditate, and will it help them?*

Yes, to both questions. Children are admitted for lessons at Transcendental Meditation centers if their parents are practicing meditators. It is only required that they be old enough to keep their mantra secret. A walking mantra is given to young children, under eleven, who might have trouble sitting still. Children can be taught to meditate when they show a desire and are willing to practice it daily. If their parents are enthusiastic meditators, they will be be more naturally interested. Benefits are similar to those of the adult, but experiences are understood at the child's maturational level. Parents who meditate can teach their children a simple method selected from those described in this book, perhaps something as simple as using the phrase "God is love" as a mantra.

15. *Could the hyperactive child be helped through meditation?*

Since meditation releases stress and tensions and fosters tranquillity, it should greatly benefit the hyperactive child. The difficulty is getting such children to sit still to meditate. A walking mantra could be used if the child is young or is willing to use a method different from that of his or her parents. To my knowledge, there is no research in progress dealing with the effects of meditation on hyperactivity. Such research could be useful in determining the extent to which meditation could benefit these children.

16. *Can meditation help a person to lose weight?*

Reducing stress in some people through meditation could result in weight loss if the person has been overeating because of stress. However, the larger number of overweight people are the victims of poor eating habits, and these will need to be changed before any weight loss can be sustained. The growth in discipline a person is experiencing through meditation may indirectly contribute to a person's ability to make a permanent change in eating habits.

Notes to Chapter 8

[1] Thomas R. Kelly, *A Testament of Devotion* (New York: Harper & Row, Publishers, 1941), p. 32.

[2] Frank J. MacHovec, *OM: A Guide to Meditation and Inner Tranquility* (New York: Peter Pauper Press, 1973), p. 10

[3] Thomas R. Kelly, *A Testament of Devotion,* p. 58.

Goals
in
Christian
Growth

Although there are many ways we grow as Christians, the following essays deal with seven basic areas of growth. They are ideals in the Christian's life, and so can serve as goals for our efforts to move ever closer to the ideal.

They are offered here as a convenient supplement to the previous chapters. They can serve as the inspirational reading suggested for preceding individual daily meditation or for reading during the study or discussion period suggested for group meditation meetings.

Loving God

"You shall love the Lord your God with all your heart, and with all your soul, and with all your mind" (Matthew 22:37).

Jesus declared this ancient Jewish law, called the Shema, the greatest of all the laws. In fact, he stated that with the second law, loving your neighbor as yourself, it was the basis for all the many Jewish laws of his day as well as for the teachings of the prophets. He placed it at the center of any religious effort. It is therefore the foundation for any plan for Christian growth that we can conceive.

Yet, as paramount as this is, God has left us free to choose to love him. We are not obligated to do so. Tagore, the great Indian poet, in his essay "Soul Consciousness" says it this way:

> It is only in this region of will that anarchy is permitted; . . . Indeed, God has stood aside from our self, where his watchful patience knows no bounds, and where he never forces open the doors if shut against him. For this self of ours has to attain its ultimate meaning, which is the soul, not through the compulsion of God's power but through love, and thus become united with God in freedom.[1]

There are various excuses we make for refusing to love God with our total being and devious ways we even evade facing the fact that we love ourselves much more. But our chance to begin this path of growth only comes when we face honestly what we correctly fear, that loving God completely will require letting go of our own egos, and this is intensely frightening.

As we move into a life of meditation and prayer, we come eventually to the intuitive knowledge that our larger self is an expression of God, and that only by letting go of our little self, the ego, can the larger self, our very soul, fulfill its destiny for expression.

But the dawning realization of this truth still lacks the direction necessary to move from a life centered in self to a life centered in love for God. Where do we begin? What steps will take us there?

There is a story told of a seeker after God who became a mendicant friar about the fifth century and wandered from village to village seeking to learn the nature of God that he might love Him properly. He studied the heavens and the changing seasons and talked with many wise people he met. But years passed, and although he was more and more awed by creation, he felt no nearer knowing the nature of God.

Then one day he wandered into a village ravaged by disease. He worked along with the villagers to ease the pain of those stricken, but hundreds died. When the sickness had passed, he discovered eleven children, now without parents, who had no relatives nor friends to care for them. He expressed to the villagers his willingness to provide for the children if they would furnish him a house and a small plot of land on which to grow food. He was given a cottage and a few acres of ground.

Ten busy years passed, and the seeker had little time for questions of philosophy. But each child became dearer to him than his own life. Then one day a lad, now sixteen and interested in the history of the village, asked him a question. "Father, why did you come to this village?"

"I was on a mission, my boy. I wanted to know the nature of God."

"And did you learn the nature of God?"

"Yes, lad, the nature of God is love."

"And, Father, who taught that to you?"

"You did, my son."

We begin to know something of the nature of God when we love. When we understand that God, creator of heaven and earth, loves us like a Father, then we know how to love him in return. As it is stated in 1 John 4:7-8: "Beloved, let us love one another, for love is of God, and he who loves is born of God and knows God. He who does not love does not know God; for God is love."

We begin our life of loving God totally by any growth in loving. All love is of God, and ultimately all love takes us to God himself.

Loving Others

"You shall love your neighbor as yourself" (Matthew 22:39).

In the two great commandments, Jesus ties together loving God, loving one's neighbor, and loving oneself. Other passages show his teaching that loving God and other people cannot be separated: "If any one says, 'I love God,' and hates his brother, he is a liar; . . . And this commandment we have from him, that he who loves God should love his brother also" (1 John 4:20-21).

Psychology is verifying the third side of this triangle, that only a person with a genuine self-esteem can freely love others.

So how do we change when we realize that we do not love people as Jesus did? We are often impatient with strangers, angry at those we love, and annoyed if our friends inconvenience us. When people seek our help, even our assistance is sometimes lacking in real love. We want their problems quickly resolved so we can return to our own concerns.

Some have suggested that loving one's neighbor as oneself means always desiring the best for him or her as we do untiringly for ourselves. Even when we do not highly regard our actions and motives, we continue working for our interests and success. This is a good standard, and it should apply in our relationship to other people, but it is difficult to desire and work for the success and happiness of someone with whom we are angry or irritated or impatient. Where do we get the necessary different attitude?

Jesus directed us to the one pathway in the first Great Commandment, loving God with our total being. Thomas Kelly suggests that we can move worshipfully into the Presence of God and be changed:

For the experience of Presence is the experience of peace, and the experience of peace is the experience not of inaction but of power, and the experience of power is the experience of a pursuing Love that loves its way untiringly to victory. He who knows the Presence knows peace, and he who knows peace knows power and walks in complete faith that the objective Power and Love which has overtaken him will overcome the world.[2]

And this power, peace, and love experienced in the Presence will change our relationship with other persons. Kelly describes this new sensitivity as a "tendering":

For the experience of an inflooding, all-enfolding Love, which is at the center of Divine Presence, is of a Love which *embraces all creation,* not just our little, petty selves. . . . There is a tendering of the soul toward *everything* in creation, from the sparrow's fall to the slave under the lash. The hard-lined face of a money-bitten financier is as deeply touching to the *tendered* soul as are the burned-out eyes of miners' children, remote and unseen victims of his so-called success. There is a sense in which, in this terrible tenderness, we become one with God and bear in our quivering souls the sins and burdens, the benightedness and the tragedy of the creatures of the whole world, and suffer in their suffering, and die in their death.[3]

If God's love is truly overflowing through us, we will truly love our neighbor as ourselves.

Loving Ourselves

"You shall love your neighbor as yourself" (Matthew 22:39).

Jesus' commandment to love our neighbor as ourselves implies that we should love ourselves by some correct high standard. At first it looks deceptively simple, and we may think we already love ourselves this way. We work diligently for our own interests. We judge much of life by how we are affected. We are usually at the center of our own universe, and our perspective of people and events is often from a very personal point of view. It would appear that we love ourselves enough.

In fact, from this viewpoint we sometimes feel a conflict between the commandment to love other people and the implication to love ourselves. The teachings about turning the other cheek, going the second mile, and taking up our cross somehow seem to tilt the balance in favor of loving other people over loving ourselves. It is a dilemma. Should we go the second mile if it grossly impinges on our own rights? Doesn't the commandment suggest that we should concern ourselves also with our own happiness as well as that of others?

Actually, seeing life from where we happen to be is a rather common way of looking at it. Most people are quite self-centered. But this doesn't necessarily indicate any kind of healthy self-love. The neurotic characterized by constant concern about himself or herself sees all of life from his or her own point of view, but this is not proper self-love.

In contrast, the inner security that stems from proper self-love allows a person to act with genuine unselfishness. Persons with an inner confirmation of their own value have no need to grasp for power, goods, status; for their worth does not depend on the securing of any of this. Their confidence in their own worth indeed makes such symbols unnecessary. And because they have a deep sense of their worth, they can give when others can't. They can look beyond their own point of view to see that of other persons. They can extend kindness and helpfulness even when it costs them something.

But where does this inner confidence, this proper self-love, come from? How do we go about securing it? The message coming over and over to us from those spiritual giants who lived close to God is that we find our value in the enfolding love of God. An inner security comes in seeking God and, as Thomas Merton says, in "being found in Him."[4]

One characteristic that impresses us in the lives of true Christian saints is their humility. Their lives testify that the more persons live in awareness of the presence of God, the less they are concerned with their own recognition and rewards. They accept with gratitude as gifts from God all that is good in themselves and in their lives. The conflict between loving themselves and others disappears with the insight that all are a part of each other and all a part of God. They seek no glory for themselves when their attention is on God and his righteousness. The high standard of loving themselves seen in such persons is their acceptance of their lives as a part of the goodness of God. They know themselves to be children of God, and they know others to be also. Their actions are in harmony. They go the second mile; they turn the other cheek, and yet they feel no loss of stature, and no resentment. They do it because they love their brothers and for love of their Father in whose enfolding love they know their place of worthiness is secure.

Living Selflessly

"Feed my sheep" (John 21:17).

When we make the decision to try seriously the Christian way, we naturally look at our present way of living to see what adjustments need to be made. Usually the change most often needed concerns our purposes. Most of our efforts have formerly been directed toward achieving personal rewards of some kind, not necessarily very selfish or unusual, but nevertheless, quite centered about ourselves. They may have been for professional achievement, for popularity, for recognition of abilities, for firmer financial security or gain, or any other quite normal goal of life.

With a determination to try the way taught by Jesus, we have to decide where now to direct our efforts. We can quickly reply that we will direct our efforts toward doing God's will rather than our own, and this is the heart of the matter, but knowing God's will for our lives is not always easy. It isn't zapped magically to us on the day we seek direction. It takes prayer and meditation and clear thinking about a standard already given to us by Jesus that will help guide us.

After the resurrection, Jesus called Peter away from his fishing again and asked him, "Simon, son of John, do you love me more than these?"

Peter's reply was unwavering. "Yes, Lord; you know that I love you."

Jesus answered this confirmation of love with three words, "Feed my lambs."

Three times Jesus asked the same question and three times, following Peter's declaration of love, he gave Peter the same directive for his life, "Feed my sheep." Peter was being called to minister to people. It is the same call that comes to anyone serious about following Jesus. Jesus' teachings repeatedly give two main guides for us to follow. Service is the goal, and love is the method. We are all ministers who seek to follow Jesus, no matter the profession.

Do our present activities and goals meet this standard of service in love? If not, can they be adjusted through the infusion of this high purpose?

A businessman works primarily to increase his sales record each year, to expand his company, to sell his product better, to make a bigger profit, and to succeed in all the normal ways of the business world. If his goal becomes ministering to people in love, he might continue more or less the same pattern of activities, but the whole purpose is elevated. Through his business, he now works to help people that God may be glorified and humankind served.

Such a standard changes any business, profession, or activity. A teacher whose purpose is to be a channel for God's love by helping his students has the Christlike direction. A lawyer becomes a greater lawyer if she works to serve humanity rather than herself. The doctor is of greater stature who seeks to serve than to be served by her profession. So it is with all the main thrusts of our lives, whether we be housewife and mother or governor or janitor.

We may feel that such a way of directing our lives is impossibly ideal. We may even think it unnatural. But we see examples of this kind of living and, because of these lives, we know the way of love which Jesus taught is possible.

Albert Schweitzer, without a doubt, could have fulfilled any personal ambition for wealth, fame, or power. His story is well known. At the age of thirty, with firmly established reputations in music and theology, he entered medical school. He felt he could best minister to humankind by relieving physical suffering. His decision took him to one of the less developed parts of Africa, where in the hot jungle he established a hospital at Lambarene, French Equatorial Africa (now Gabon).

Is there no lesser standard for those of us who would like to live the Christian way by a less difficult route? No, there is but one standard that Jesus gave for life, that of service in love.

The difficulty is not in seeing the pathway, but accepting it for our lives. Once we decide to follow the way, the first step is apparent, and each succeeding step is seen as we walk this way. Jesus offered abundant life to followers of the way and promised to be with us always as we move out in faith.

Living by Faith—Without Anxiety

"Therefore I tell you, do not be anxious about your life"
(Matthew 6:25).

Among the hardest of Jesus' teachings for us to take seriously are those about not being anxious. "Therefore I tell you, do not be anxious about your life," he said to the disciples as he reminded them of the Father's care of the birds of the air and the lilies of the field. "Therefore do not be anxious about tomorrow, for tomorrow will be anxious for itself. Let the day's own trouble be sufficient for the day" (Matthew 6:34). This looks to us, if not impossible, quite impractical, surely lacking in the foresight needed for successful living.

We are trained from the beginning of life to be competitive in the race for success. The prizes we seek are recognition, material possessions, and power. We measure our total life's worth by the size of these accumulations. And this program for living has made us into a nation of pill-takers with a mounting array of physical problems: heart attacks, ulcers, high blood pressure, mental and emotional setbacks.

Jesus gave us a key to not being anxious. He said, "Seek first his kingdom and his righteousness, and all these things shall be yours as well" (Matthew 6:33). He didn't pretend that we have no physical needs, but he stressed centering our lives in God and his righteousness to put things in proper perspective. Most of our seeking for material possessions has gone far beyond our actual needs. They are part of that image of success we are projecting to convince ourselves as well as others of our real worth. We are seeking first the kingdom of our own success, and we cannot seem to accumulate enough to convince us that we have arrived. But when we truly seek God's kingdom and his righteousness, we begin to see clearly the tinsel toys to which we have been devoting our lives. And as we begin to experience the presence of God through prayer and meditation, there comes a growing awareness of the fantastic truth that God loves us just as we are. We don't have to become company president, accumulate wealth, or even attain a life of great goodness. We are already infinitely valuable in God's sight. This knowledge brings the inner security that we have been trying and failing to attain through our own efforts.

But some of our anxiety stems from concern about those we hold dearest. Will our children weather the perils of growing up in today's irreverent society; will our husband return safely from his business trip to Tokyo; will our brother finish the racing season without injury? Our loved ones face real perils each day, and it is difficult not to worry about them. Yet, even this less self-centered anxiety shows a lack of faith in the loving concern and care of the Father for us.

Analyzing our worrying habit quickly shows that fortunately most of the things we worry about never happen. Even the few that do were not helped by our worrying. The futility of the anxiety is obvious, but the results of anxiety both in the lives of the worrier and those being worried about is not so obvious.

Jesus firmly instructed us to live in the present. "Let the day's own trouble be sufficient for the day." In truth, we know there is no other possibility. The future cannot be touched in the present, and the past is forever beyond our control. And only by giving our full attention to the present do we fully live each day. And, of course, our future is determined by how we live today.

Jesus never promised that we would be shielded from the problems of life, but he did promise to be with us.

We have no need for anxiety. God has promised us abundant life in the present and an eternal future. With faith in these two promises, we can face without anxiety the events of life as we seek day by day the kingdom of God and his righteousness.

Living the Disciplined Life

"Take my yoke upon you, and learn from me" (Matthew 11:29).

When we talk about living the joyous life, the loving life, or a life free from fear and anxiety, we are attracted. We want such a life. But when we think of living a disciplined life, we are immediately apprehensive. We wonder if anything that sounds so austere is necessary. We want no part of it.

Yet Christian growth requires effort on our part. Although all the blessings of God are freely given, a response on our part is necessary for their reception. We get the word "discipline" from the Latin word for learning, from which word also comes our word for disciple. The spiritual life can only be maintained by those willing to make the effort for inner growth. And perception and appreciation of the spiritual realities can only come through discipline. Only someone who has studied music can fully appreciate the beauty of a Bach chorale.

Some might think that such growth would come automatically with meditation and prayer, and there is much truth to this. By faithfully observing our time for prayer and meditation, we will be more naturally inclined to a disciplined life.

However, just keeping our daily commitment to the time chosen for our devotional life requires discipline, and the meditator will notice how often other things seem to interfere with this block of time. There seem to be counter desires embedded within wanting no regimentation, no regulation.

Actually there are many reasons why discipline comes hard. Inertia and the comfortableness of living with our old ways, fear of change, and tenacity of old habits all play their part. But when we look at our resistances squarely, we see that the real battle is one of allegiance. We do not want to relinquish center stage. With our free wills, God's great gift to us which marks our humanity, we stubbornly hang onto that most familiar part of ourselves, our ego. Our self-indulgence, whether with time, food, drink, possessions, worry, self-pity, or whatever, is our way of saying, "Me, me, me." We allow the antics of the ego to block the full expression of the soul.

Even when we commit our lives to God and try to get ourselves offstage, we find that we are creatures of habit. The old habits, the expressions of a self-centered life, keep repeating themselves almost automatically. We find it difficult replacing them with new habits of the God-centered life. We know how Paul felt when he said, "For I do not do what I want, but I do the very thing I hate" (Romans 7:15).

How do we exchange the old habits for the new? The truth is that there are no shortcuts, no magic formulas that make it happen quickly. It takes time and effort and firm commitment.

Once the famous sculptor Rodin was asked by a tourist if it were difficult to sculpt. "Not at all, Madam," replied the master. "You simply buy a block of marble and chip away what you don't want."[5]

By keeping ourselves in growing awareness of God's presence through meditation and prayer, we are making the necessary first step. Then, by chipping away those old habits of self-indulgent, self-centered living, we will gradually find that God is doing his work of redemption through us in ways we never dreamed possible. For, as it is written in John 1:12, "But to all who received him . . . he gave power to become children of God."

Living Joyously

"These things I have spoken to you, that my joy may be in you, and that your joy may be full" (John 15:11).

To be happy, to experience joy, meaning, fulfillment is a universal desire. In spite of widespread knowledge that this is a basic motivating factor in human behavior and the industrious commercial effort to cash in on this fact, not enough real joy is being experienced today. Any daily newspaper testifies to the lack of joy in the lives of too many people. We suspect that the realization of joy is not in proportion to the efforts being made to attain it. We are painfully aware that even in an affluent society real joy can't be purchased, and we are frustrated because happiness seems to elude us when we pursue it most fervently.

Yet many of the teachers from the East teach that our natural state of existence is bliss. And our idioms show that we believe this, for when we are worried or upset, we say, "I'm not myself today." We recognize that we express our true selves best when we are free and happy.

Jesus had some penetrating things to say about happiness. He said that he came into the world that we might "have life and have it more abundantly." Wanting to be happy, then, is not out of line with the Christian life. Indeed, if we are not living a life full of joy, we can suspect that we have missed the basic message of Jesus.

The teachings of Jesus which deal directly with happiness are called the Beatitudes. Yet they are puzzling. Jesus describes the happy, or blessed, person as one who is poor in spirit, who mourns for God, who is meek, who hungers and thirsts after righteousness, who is merciful, who seeks to make peace, and who is persecuted for righteousness' sake. These do not sound like the conditions of a fulfilled person. They sound more like descriptions of a person deprived even of a satisfying relationship with God.

Yet, on closer inspection, two types emerge. The Beatitudes appear to be related to two kinds of activity: seeking a closer relationship with God and expressing in life the results of such a relationship. Those who consider themselves poor in spirit, who mourn for God, or who hunger and thirst for righteousness are those who are earnestly seeking a greater realization of God's presence in their lives. Jesus' teachings about the success of this search is without equivocation. "Theirs is the kingdom of heaven." "They shall be comforted." "They shall be satisfied."

The other Beatitudes describe those who express the God-filled life. They are humble, merciful, pure in heart, peacemakers, and courageous even in the face of persecution. Their promise of blessedness is also firm. They shall inherit the earth, obtain mercy, see God, and be called the sons of God. Theirs is the kingdom of heaven.

Jesus is describing a life of great happiness. Other teachings of Jesus reaffirm this pathway of seeking first God and his righteousness and then living the results of that relationship. The two Great Commandments underscore this pathway for the disciple.

It is no wonder, then, that we fail so often to find the joy in life that we want. We look for joy everywhere except in the presence of God. We frequently ask God to help us obtain the things we believe necessary for our happiness, but seldom are aware that it is the relationship with the Father himself that brings the joy.

Yet even here we find a problem, for to seek God for our own selfish purposes, even our happiness, is to lose him. The joy only comes when we seek him because we love him. Evelyn Underhill discusses this in her book *Mysticism:*

> The mystic does not enter on his quest because he desires the happiness of the Beatific Vision, the ecstasy of union with the Absolute, or any other personal reward. . . .
>
> "O Love," said St. Catherine of Genoa, "I do not wish to follow thee for sake of these delights, but solely from the motive of true love." Those who do otherwise are only, in the plain words of St. John of the Cross, "spiritual gluttons": or, in the milder metaphor here adopted, magicians of the more high-minded sort.[6]

If we seek God for the happiness he gives, it will elude us. If we seek God for love of him, he will find us, and our joy will be complete.

Notes for
"Goals in Christian Growth"

[1] Rabindranath Tagore, *Sadhana—The Realization of Life* (New York: The Macmillan Publishing Co., Inc., 1915), p. 42.

[2] Thomas R. Kelly, *A Testament of Devotion* (New York: Harper & Row, Publishers, 1941), pp. 102-103.

[3] *Ibid.,* p. 106.

[4] Thomas Merton, *Life and Holiness* (New York: Herder and Herder, 1963), p. 31.

[5] William R. Parker, Elaine St. Johns Dare, *Prayer Can Change Your Life* (Englewood Cliffs, N.J.: Prentice-Hall, Inc., 1957), p. 119.

[6] Thomas S. Kepler, *The Evelyn Underhill Reader* (Nashville: Abingdon Press, 1962), p. 36.

Guided Meditations

The guided meditations in this section are planned for group use. They are to be followed by a fifteen-minute period of silence. They should be read slowly and quietly and with pauses at the appropriate places. Any instructions for a particular selection should be followed. As suggested earlier in the book, they may be taped for use by individuals.

Before beginning any group meditation, the group should prepare physically with a few seconds of deep breathing and a short period of consciously relaxing all parts of the body. The body should be made as comfortable as possible.

For Renewal

This meditation is more effective if read by two readers. One reader should read the quoted material and the other should read the responses. The quoted material should be read a little more forcefully than the responses. The quoted material is from Isaiah 40 and Genesis 1 and 2. It is in italics to distinguish it more easily.

"But they who wait for the Lord
Shall renew their strength."

We wait in the silence.
We wait. (pause)

"The Lord God . . . breathed into [man]
The breath of life,
And man became a living being."

We breathe the breath of God's Spirit
Into our lives.   (pause)

"They shall mount up with wings like eagles."

We breathe into our lives God's power.
We breathe out our weakness.   (pause)

"They shall run and not be weary."

We breathe into our lives God's strength to endure.
We breathe out our fatigue.   (pause)

"They shall walk and not faint."

We breathe into our lives God's joyful activity.
We breathe out our unconcern.   (pause)

"God said, 'Let us make man in our image,
After our likeness.'"

We wait in the silence; we wait.   (pause)

Make us in thy image.
Breathe into our lives
Thy power to create all that is good,
Thy power to love.
Make us in thy image.
We wait in the silence; we wait.

(The period of silence)

For Guidance

The world is filled with holy energy.
All matter pulsates with life.
The plant prospers according to design,
Growing purposefully in its source.

Our lives are filled with holy energy;
Our lives are filled with directing light.
We are surrounded by life eternal,
Encompassing, penetrating, available.

Our feet are illumined in the light.
Divine energy directs our steps.
See the brightness about your feet.
Feel the tingle of new life.

See the radiant light about your legs.
You can move in the path of righteousness,
You can walk in the light;
You can follow the way of love.

See your arms surrounded by the light.
Feel the surge of energy renew your strength.
You can reach out to another;
You can help carry his burden.

The radiant light vibrates with the beat of your heart,
Purifying your affections.

You can love with godly caring,
And with joyful self-abandonment.

The radiant light fills your head,
Divine energy clarifies your thinking.
You see now clearly etched
The way of love and caring.

Life is filled with holy energy,
Life is filled with directing light.
Surrender now into the center of your being,
Your center of holy energy,
Your center of directing light.
Follow the leading of the light.
The pathway it illumines
Can be followed with confidence,
Can be followed with peace,
Can be followed with joy,

For the holy energy filling us is love;
The directing light leading us is love;
And God who is all is love.

(The period of silence)

For Healing

The plan for this guided meditation should be explained to the group before beginning. Members should sit in a circle. Those who want healing should sit in the center of the circle. If someone desires healing for someone not present, he should sit in the circle representing that person.

The first part of the meditation script should be read, followed by the silence. When the reader begins again, members should focus their attention on those in the center of the circle. Each member should try to tune him/herself mentally to the one being healed, attempting to feel a unity with the person. In turn following the leader, each member should stand and place his or her hands on the person or persons and make the following statement: "May love and healing flow through me to you." When all have done this, with hands still on one being healed, the prayer given is prayed, the members repeating each line after the leader.

The Healing Meditation

Silence fills this place.
Silence surrounds us.
Silence quiets our thinking.
Silence settles into us.
We are still.

In the stillness there is life.
In the stillness there is energy.
In the stillness there is healing.
In the stillness there is God.

We open ourselves to the silence.
We merge with the energy flowing through us.
We rest in the Being of God.
We are still.

(Fifteen minutes of silence)

In the stillness there is life.
In the stillness there is energy.
In the energy there is healing.
In the healing there is love.
And in love there is God.

Leader rises, places hands on one to be healed and says: "May love and healing flow through me to you."

Each person in turn repeats the action and statement of the leader. All hands remain on a person in the healing center during the prayer which follows.

LEADER: We thank you, Father,
For the blessings of healing,
For the blessings of wholeness
Received here today. Amen.

(Members of group repeat each line of the prayer after the leader.)

For Acceptance

This meditation can be used by groups as a guided meditation. It is also planned for taping for individual use, and all parts suggested for the devotional time are included. It is to be read slowly with pauses at the designated places. The words in parentheses are instructions or references and should not be taped. For individual use, first person plural words in the meditation and prayers should be changed to first person singular.

(Prayer)   We praise thee, Father, for thy steadfast love that endures forever.

(pause)

(Inspirational Reading)   Hear now and consider these words from Psalm 139:

O Lord, thou hast searched me and known me!
Thou knowest when I sit down and when I rise up;
   thou discernest my thoughts from afar.
Thou searchest out my path and my lying down,
   and art acquainted with all my ways.
Even before a word is on my tongue,
   lo, O Lord, thou knowest it altogether.
Thou dost beset me behind and before,
   and layest thy hand upon me.
Such knowledge is too wonderful for me;
   it is high; I cannot attain it.
Whither shall I go from thy Spirit?
   Or whither shall I flee from they presence?
If I ascend to heaven, thou art there!
   If I make my bed in Sheol, thou art there!
If I take the wings of the morning and dwell in the
   uttermost parts of the sea,
   even there thy hand shall lead me,
   and thy right hand shall hold me.
If I say, "Let only darkness cover me,
   and the light about me be night,"
even the darkness is not dark to thee,
   the night is bright as the day;

for darkness is as light with thee.

(pause)

(Meditation)

We rest in the knowledge that all our thoughts, our dreams, our hopes, our ways are known by you, Heavenly Father.

(pause)

We feel your hand upon us, supporting, accepting us.

(pause)

We cherish your constant presence with us and your complete understanding of us.

(pause)

We return the comforting love encircling us.

(pause)

We accept the leading of your Spirit.

(pause)

In your presence, Father, we renounce our frantic efforts to earn your love. We accept your love for us already given.

(pause)

We renounce attempts to prove our worthiness by rating ourselves higher than our sister and brother. We accept your love for us already given.

(pause)

We renounce our struggle to be considered important.
We accept your love for us already given.

(pause)

We renounce our frequent preoccupation with our own unworthiness. We accept your judgment that crowns us with your love and acceptance.
We accept your knowing us and your love for us already given.

(pause)

Now let us move into God's creative silence using the word

"love," another name for God, to carry us deeply into his presence. Let the word "love" repeat itself in your thoughts.

(fifteen minutes of silence)

(Intercessory Prayer) Heavenly Father, we praise you for the love you so freely give to your children. Let us now become channels of your love and healing to these, your children.

(Leave enough time here when taping to allow a list of names to be read)

(Closing Prayer) O give thanks to the Lord, for he is good,
for his steadfast love endures for ever.

O give thanks to the God of gods,
for his steadfast love endures for ever.

O give thanks to the Lord of lords,
for his steadfast love endures for ever.
Amen (Psalm 136:1-3).

For Reaching Goals

This is a visualization meditation. Members of the group should sit with eyes closed and follow the fantasy as it is read, allowing free rein to their imagination.

You see yourself on a circular drive lined with pine and cedar trees. You are approaching a small chapel of native stone. With a sense of excitement, you hurry to the entrance. As you approach the door, it opens, and you are met by a tall man, dressed in a white robe and illumined by an unseen light. He greets you with outstretched hands which you clasp.

You and he seem to know the purpose of the meeting, and he leads you into a bright, sunny carpeted room. He kneels momentarily at an altar located immediately inside the room. You pause with him.

(slight pause)

He then leads you on into the room. It is a pleasant room with green potted ferns in the corners and a large window with a comfortable chair nearby which you are invited to take. You sit down. The guide hands you a pad of paper and a pen. You are told to write down one or two of your most important goals. They may be any kind of goals: social, professional, or spiritual. There are only two requirements. They must be worthy of your best self and they must be for yourself, not for someone else. They must be your own dreams which you hold at the present time.

You take the pen and begin writing.

(three minutes of silence)

The guide returns and hands you an envelope. You fold the paper and put in into the envelope. The guide instructs you to seal the envelope and carry it to the altar at the entrance to the room. In front of the altar there is a cushioned kneeling bench. You kneel and place your envelope on the altar.

(one minute of silence)

You are now led to another room, a long, rectangular room with shelves on all sides. The guide directs you to a desk and hands you a long blank sheet of paper. You are told to list anything you feel essential for reaching the goals you have chosen. You take the requisition slip and write down the things you need to accomplish your goals.

(three minutes of silence)

You are told that these necessities for your work will be delivered to you at the time you need them. You are led from this storeroom to a room adjoining it nearby. It is simply furnished with a couch and pillows in one corner. You are told to rest until the guide returns. You lie on the couch, adjust the pillows, and feel yourself relax. You think of the goals you have offered on the altar to God. You become very sleepy. You feel yourself fading off into sleep.

As you sleep, you see yourself. You realize that you are dreaming, but the dream is very real. You see yourself beginning a program to work for your dreams. You see yourself progress. As though you were watching a movie, you watch the story unfold as you move successfully to achieve the goals so recently formulated on paper.

(three minutes of silence)

You are aware that the guide has returned. You stand up and indicate that you are ready. Wordlessly you follow him from the room to the room with the altar. He bids you good-bye with a smile, and you are alone. You see again the kneeling bench on which you recently knelt to offer your dreams to God. You kneel again. You are suddenly filled with assurance and joy. You thank God that the goals you set for yourself can be accomplished. You thank God for their accomplishment.

(one minute of silence)

You leave the chapel with faith and joy in your heart.

Bibliography

For further study, the following resources are recommended.

On Meditation

Baker, M. E. Penny, *Meditation: A Step Beyond with Edgar Cayce.* New York: Pinnacle Books, 1975.

Bloomfield, Harold H.; Cain, Michael Peter; and Jaffe, Dennis T., *TM: Discovering Inner Energy and Overcoming Stress.* New York: Delacorte Press, imprint of Dell Publishing Co., Inc., 1975.

Forem, Jack, *Transcendental Meditation.* New York: E. P. Dutton & Co., Inc., 1974.

Goldsmith, Joel S., *The Art of Meditation.* New York: Harper & Row, Publishers, 1956.

LeShan, Lawrence, *How to Meditate: A Guide to Self-Discovery.* New York: Bantam Books, Inc., 1975.

Paulson, J. Sig, and Dickerson, Ric, "The Miracle of Creative Meditation" in three cassettes. A taped conversation between the minister of Unity Village Chapel and a scientist, M.D., Ph. D. Can be ordered from Unity, Lee Summit, Missouri.

Progoff, Ira, *The Well and the Cathedral*. New York: Dialogue House Library, 1971.

―――, *The White Robed Monk*. New York: Dialogue House Library, 1972.

―――, *The Star-Cross*. New York: Dialogue House Library, 1971. (All guided meditations, called Cycles of Process Meditation.)

White, John, ed., *What Is Meditation?* Garden City, N.Y.: Anchor Press, imprint of Doubleday Publishing Company, 1974.

On Mysticism

Harkness, Georgia, *Mysticism: Its Meaning and Message*. Nashville: Abingdon Press, 1973.

Stace, Walter T., *The Teachings of the Mystics*. New York: Mentor Book, imprint of The New American Library, Inc., 1960.

Underhill, Evelyn, *The Mystics of the Church*. New York: Schocken Books Inc., 1964.

―――, *The Essentials of Mysticism*. New York: E. P. Dutton & Co., 1960.

―――, *Mysticism*. New York: E. P. Dutton & Co., Inc., 1961.

For the Devotional Life

New books helpful to the devotional life are constantly being published. The meditator is encouraged to investigate them, which he or she can easily do as they are readily available in any religious book store. Many of the books listed below are older ones that have proved their worth through the years.

Asquith, Glenn H., *Footprints in the Sand.* Valley Forge: Judson Press, 1975.

Baille, John, *A Diary of Private Prayer.* New York: Charles Scribner's Sons, 1949.

Johnson, Orien, *Becoming Transformed.* Valley Forge: Judson Press, 1973.

Kelly, Thomas R., *A Testament of Devotion.* New York: Harper & Row, Publishers, 1941.

Laubach, Frank C., *Prayer, the Mightiest Force in the World.* Old Tappan, N.J.: Spire Books, imprint of Fleming H. Revell Company, 1959.

Lawrence, Brother, *The Practice of the Presence of God.* Old Tappan, N.J.: Spire Books, imprint of Fleming H. Revell Company, 1958.

Lewis, C. S., *Letters to Malcolm: Chiefly on Prayer.* New York: Harcourt Brace Jovanovich, Inc., 1964.

Merton, Thomas, *Contemplative Prayer.* New York: Herder and Herder, Inc., 1969.

Miller, Keith, *The Taste of New Wine.* Waco, Tex.: Word, Inc., 1965.

O'Connor, Elizabeth, *Search for Silence.* Waco, Tex.: Word, Inc., 1972.

Phillips, J. B., *For This Day.* Edited by Denis Duncan. Waco, Tex.: Word, Inc., 1975.

Schweitzer, Albert, *Reverence for Life.* New York: Harper & Row, Publishers, 1969.

Swami Prabhavananda, *The Sermon on the Mount According to Vedanta.* Hollywood, Calif.: Vedanta Press, 1963.

Tagore, Rabindranath, *Sadhana, the Realization of Life.* Tucson, Ariz.: Omen Press, 1972.

Thomas a Kempis, *The Imitation of Christ.* Garden City, N.Y.: Image Books, imprint of Doubleday & Co., 1955.

p. 59
p. 63
p. 71-2